David Brayshaw was 47 when he decided to leave his comfortable job in the City for ever – and his wife and four children for seven weeks – to attempt to become the first person to drive from London to Beijing via the Trans-Siberian Highway. He was not a competent mechanic. In fact he had no particular skills that were especially suited to a venture such as this. To make things harder, he drove a 1960 Austin Healey sports car and chose to go with a man he had barely met before. Predictably, he and Nawal Saighal encountered many obstacles on their 8,000-mile journey, including some that literally forced the car off the road.

Fortunately, Siberian drivers were helpful and stopped to assist the travellers, on one occasion entertaining them with a sauna and a family feast until the car was roadworthy again. In a journey of many surprises they met scores of friendly and hospitable locals – and several inordinately obstructive bureaucrats. Being told, at gunpoint, that they could not cross the border into China and must 'Go back to Moscow' after 4,500 miles could have been the last straw, but determination and diplomacy are hard to beat.

David Brayshaw was born in Yorkshire and educated at a grammar school there and later in Hertfordshire. He began working in banking locally, and then moved to an exciting and successful career in the international money markets in the City. Faced with early retirement in 1996, while still in his forties, he took 'the road to Beijing' and wrote this account of his epic journey. He is now a financial consultant, advising governments and international banks. Married to Jenny, he has four children and lives in Hertfordshire.

THE ROAD TO BEIJING

David Brayshaw

The Book Guild Ltd
Sussex, England

The Book Guild Ltd.
25 High Street,
Lewes, Sussex

First published 2000
© David Brayshaw 2000

Set in Times
Typesetting by
SetSystems Ltd, Saffron Walden, Essex

Printed in Great Britain by
Athenaeum Press Ltd, Gateshead

A catalogue record for this book is
available from the British Library

ISBN 1 85776 403 X

CONTENTS

Prologue   vii

1   The Beginning   1

2   The Dream Takes Shape   7

3   Preparation   14

4   Across Europe   37

5   Siberia   73

6   The Sino-Soviet Border   132

7   China   148

    Routing Details   175

    Acknowledgements   177

PROLOGUE

'We are witnessing a country on the verge of collapse. You must recognise that law and order has already broken down outside the main cities. It really is very dangerous at the moment so I would strongly advise you not to drive across Russia by car. If you insist then you must follow these basic guidelines: avoid looking conspicuous; don't stop for anything; don't drive alone – wait for another couple of cars and form a convoy and, most importantly, never ever drive at night.'

I often thought about this advice given to me by a senior American diplomat based in Moscow. It seemed very sensible at the time. I thought about it again one week later as I lay underneath our highly conspicuous Austin Healey (the only one in the country?) all alone and stationary in the middle of the night, deep in a Siberian forest as we attempted, yet again, to repair the exhaust. What on earth was I doing here, I wondered – as I tried not to think about bandits lurking in the rustling forest nearby.

We had set out from England in a 1960 Austin Healey sports car in an attempt to drive from London to Beijing. Unbeknown to us, we were about to enter the record books. We would be the first people ever to drive from London to Beijing via the Trans-Siberian 'highway' entering China at the first possible border point at Manzhouli, Inner Mongolia.

It was the summer of 1996 and just a few days before the Russian presidential elections. The country was in a highly charged and nervous state. A return to hardline communism under the contender Mr Zuganov or continuing reforms under the incumbent Mr Yeltsin? Civil unrest was forecast for either eventuality. As well as having to struggle with rough roads and uncertain supplies of essentials such as petrol and food, we therefore also had to pay some attention to the rapidly rising crime rate – particularly in armed highway robbery.

What on earth *was* I doing there? I was a middle-aged professional living a comfortable existence with my wife and family in south-east England – which at those moments appealed immensely. I was no adventurer. I wasn't even a competent mechanic. I had never done anything like this before. . .and yet. . .and yet. . .I had to confess I had secretly nurtured a desire to do something just a little adventurous for a long time. The next few weeks turned out to be the most fascinating of my life. I wouldn't have missed the many varied and unusual experiences for anything!

1

The Beginning

I had always wanted to do at least one thing in my life that was a little different from the normal routine. Perhaps many people feel like this. Whatever the dream there are many obstacles. Lack of confidence or finance perhaps? There are many reasons why the dream often remains a dream. Perhaps the biggest difficulty for most people is the practical problem of committing oneself to several weeks away from the responsibilities of job, wife, children or parents. I was lucky. When my City firm was the subject of a takeover and I lost my job after 25 years, it proved to be a blessing in disguise. There I was at 47 – old enough at last to afford to take a little time out and yet young enough (and fit enough?) to want an adventurous interlude.

I had become increasingly disillusioned with my City life. Like many others during the eighties I was a 'potential high-flyer', maybe even classified as a yuppie a few years ago – but now the novelty and excitement of wheeling and dealing in millions had worn off. There was more to life than watching prices go up and down on VDU screens even if the financial rewards were good when one was able to forecast events correctly. I had seen too many of my friends sell their souls to this business and spend long hours, with few holidays, concentrating on keeping their jobs and out-witting the competition – and the competition came from individuals within the firm as well as from the more obvious external sources. Pressures increased over the years and as a result many had fallen by the wayside, succumbing to the demon drink, becoming victims of broken marriages, suffering health problems such as heart attacks or simply burning out at a young age – nothing left but a big bank balance. Sometimes not even that. But anyway, what good was a pile of money at that stage?

These were the sort of thoughts that I had reflected on in recent years and so I was in a receptive frame of mind when it became increasingly obvious to me that my own future prospects looked decidedly uncertain. The money market business was going through one of those periodic occasions when profits were hard to come by. Any chief executive worth his salt would quickly rush to cut costs in these conditions. I was on the main board of the company and so shared overall accountability but my day-to-day responsibility at that time was to run one of our subsidiary companies. A rule change in market practice heralded the end of the specialised business of this particular subsidiary, so I would soon be left with no power base from which to argue my case had I wished to stay. In my youth I had been extremely ambitious. By that time, however, my personal ambitions had largely been realised and, if the truth be told, my heart was no longer in it. I suspect my colleagues realised this. I saw an opportunity to negotiate a reasonable financial package for what I believed was my inevitable departure – provided I grasped it there and then. My thinking had originally been to stay at least until my early fifties but with the opportunity coming earlier, I judged that the optimum moment had arrived. Maybe I was wrong but at least one thing I had learned in the City dealing rooms had been how to make quick decisions. I had a series of protracted but friendly discussions with the chief executive. Unlike many contemporary financial firms in the City, we had never paid large bonuses but we did have a splendid pension plan which kicked in at the age of 55. It was possible to negotiate a 'reasonable' pension deal from the age of 50. Fortunately this was the way it went and the deal was struck. I walked out of the door two weeks before my forty-eighth birthday. I had to finance myself for two years but I had already saved sufficient cash (just!) to enable me to do that. Thereafter I would receive a guaranteed income

2

for life. I had still to find out whether this would be enough but at the very least I could now afford to take a prolonged sabbatical if I wished. It was a wonderful feeling to know that for the first time in my life I was financially independent.

My wife, Jenny, had been a tremendous supporter of mine through all the many years of varied fortunes at work. The last couple of years had been particularly difficult for me for a variety of reasons – some of my own making. I am the sort of person who brings problems and frustrations home with him. As a result she had suffered a lot in recent months because I had relived the daily dramas of board-room politics at home. When I announced that I was likely to leave the company she was therefore able to temper her concerns that I would be under her feet with a feeling of relief that I would perhaps, at long last, learn to relax a little.

Of our four children, Daniel was then in the final year of a university language course, Jill at secretarial college. Our two youngest, Victoria (14) and Michael (11), were still at school.

During the period that I had been arranging to leave my job, the whole subject of driving a car to China was beginning to emerge as a serious possibility. I believe in fate. Perhaps I absorbed this trait from Jenny, who is Irish. I had always wanted to go on some form of 'adventure' – ideally a journey by car to some unusual place. Was it just coincidence that for the first time in my life all the conditions necessary to do just that had emerged?

I had been interested in classic cars for many years. In particular I loved the old British sports cars made in that era when 'British built' was a guarantee of a first-class product, not least when it came to cars – there were none finer. My own particular favourite was the Austin Healey. In its day it was one up from the early MGs but perhaps not as swanky as the Jaguar XK series. The Healey 100s and the later 3000s were, in my view, the result of a perfect partnership between the skills and flair of Donald Healey and the mass-production techniques and cost savings of the mighty Austin car company. My first sports car years ago, when in my early twenties, had been a 1963 Austin Healey Sprite Mark 2. Ever since, I had coveted one of the larger Healeys – but it was not to be for many years. Like many people I had a mortgage to repay and children to clothe and feed so the buying of 'toys' had to wait.

But eventually the day did come when I could afford to look around seriously with a view to buying. Although I loved cars I knew very little of what went on under the bonnet and even less about what hidden dangers to look for when purchasing a 35-year-old classic. I contacted the Austin Healey Club and spoke to the secretary of my local area, Pete Taylor. It was clear that, at least in this part of southeast England on the Herts and Essex borders, there was a thriving Healey club with many knowledgeable and enthusiastic members. He put me in touch with a colourful character called Tony Elsoff, who lived in Suffolk. Tony was an accredited expert and was happy to accompany me when viewing Healeys for sale, in return for expenses and a modest fee – plus a decent lunch! I was keen on the latest model: the Mark 3 or BJ8 as it is more accurately know, in AH circles. The first two we saw didn't live up to their owners' descriptions. This was in 1990 and prices for classic cars had collapsed from the dizzy peaks reached a couple of years earlier to more sensible and sustainable levels. However, the earlier high prices had encouraged many people to dig out old rust heaps and complete rapid and highly suspect renovation jobs in order to reap huge rewards. One had to be very careful to avoid these.

Tony suggested that I thought about the Mark 1s. He knew of one recently reimported into England from the US, where it had originally been registered in 1960. It had spent all its life in San Francisco and, with the generally arid climate of California, was therefore less likely to be rust prone. I wasn't keen at first but that was probably due to lack of familiarity with these earlier models. It is true that the latest models had many enhancements to keep up with the competition of the day: wind-up windows and walnut veneer dashboards etc. However, there was a view among purists that these features were turning the car into something that was not originally intended. The Healey was supposed to be a basic, inexpensive, raw and unsophisticated car with a simple but sturdy engine and capable of topping 100 m.p.h. That concept was personified in the Mark 1s and never bettered. This is, of course, a view about which there is always considerable discussion in Healey circles and there is no correct answer. It all depends on personal taste as to which is the 'better' car. However, I was sold on the concept of the original 3000 and went up to Norfolk to visit the man who was to end up taking virtually a year to lovingly and painstakingly complete the ground up restoration – Bernie Clover.

He was a real craftsman of the old order. I fell in love with the car the moment I set eyes on her and visited almost every weekend throughout the year, watching progress as it developed. Bernie ended up doing a truly excellent job.

Eventually the car was delivered to my home amid great ceremony and I was like a boy with a new bicycle! I really got to know the car and its performance capabilities and was impressed from the outset with its simplicity, ruggedness and sheer power. However, one did have to remember that it was built in a bygone era. It came into its own on country B roads but was overtaken with ease on motorways when rattling along, quite literally, at 90 m.p.h. by any one of the modern-day hatchbacks that are now so popular.

My relationship with ESK193 was not just a short-lived romance but one that lasted many years. Indeed it is still a well-loved member of the family. Through the local Austin Healey club Jenny and I enjoyed many outings and events and, despite my limited technical skills, these included several long weekends in France, Belgium or Holland as well as many in England. Every so often a bit fell off or decided not to work but, then again, that also seems to happen to the owner from time to time these days, so perhaps the car and I had a lot in common! The long and the short of it was that, although the car had a strong personality all of its own, it was generally well behaved. It lived up to its reputation as a simple and tough machine and rarely let us down. We had a lot of fun in it.

2

The Dream Takes Shape

It was my old friend Pete Taylor, then the membership secretary of the Austin Healey Club, who heard I was about to leave my job and was looking for something adventurous to do. He told me that someone called Nawal Saighal had been talking about a long-distance Healey trip – perhaps I should talk to him. Nawal Saighal (pronounced 'novel sigh-gull') was, as the name might suggest, of Indian origin and a very interesting character he proved to be. He lived in St Albans, the other side of the county to me. Being a Healey owner, he was an occasional visitor to club events – but I had actually never met him before. He already had something of a reputation as an adventurer because three years earlier he had organised a posse of six classic cars on a journey to Moscow and back. The original organiser had 'disappeared' (with most of the funds, apparently) part-way through the organisational stage and it says something of Nawal's character that he was the one who kept the 'show on the road' quite literally and became the team leader. In the event only two of the cars returned in a fit state and two didn't return at all!

By coincidence Nawal had a Mark 1 1960 Healey, very similar to mine except that his was the 2+2 version whereas mine was a pure two-seater. In Healey parlance mine was a BN7 and his a BT7. Apart from the BT7 having a small shelf at the back (described as two seats in the handbook!) whereas the BN7 had less space in the cockpit but a bigger boot, our two cars looked identical, even down to the colour – Healey blue (naturally!).

I met Nawal for the first time at the annual Eastern

Centre Healey dinner-dance held at Cambridge in December of 1995. I made a particular point of talking to him and he explained his thinking. Having enjoyed the challenge and thrill of the Moscow trip a couple of years earlier, he told me that he had promised himself an exciting trip every three years. He was a sales manager at the local office of Allied Dunbar and felt he could get a few weeks off occasionally, but not too frequently. He was not absolutely certain as to his next destination but Beijing seemed the front runner in his thinking. Beijing also appealed to me as being perhaps the furthest major destination one could achieve solely on land and therefore the 'ultimate' trip. It also sounded somewhat exotic! Nawal was aiming to set off in the spring or early summer of the next year. He had done a little bit of work on the route but that was about it. I expressed a general interest and talked to him for about half an hour.

The next stage occurred when I read a brief article by Nawal in the January edition of the monthly Healey Owner's Club magazine. He was simply advertising for a companion to act as navigator on a 'trip of a lifetime' to Beijing. I called him up and then went round to his house in St Albans, about an hour or so from where I lived in Bishop's Stortford. I don't know what I expected but, surprisingly, there wasn't that much more to be said when I got there. We looked briefly at maps. I asked a number of questions like 'what happens if we have an accident in the middle of a remote Siberian forest and find ourselves lying there with broken legs or concussed?' Nawal had no reply and, indeed, nor had I. We then parted company with me being asked to draw up a detailed route and to consider how we could raise money for the trip and for the charity that we were supporting: Children in Crisis.

I still wasn't 100 per cent sure if this was right for me but as there was a long time to go before the actual 'off', a commitment at that stage seemed, illogically no doubt, somewhat easier to make. I talked it over with my wife who seemed even keener for me to go than I was myself. (There must be some moral here somewhere but perhaps best not to dwell on it!) Jenny's argument was that I had had a somewhat depressing year or two and was constantly talking about blowing away the cobwebs by doing something different. This proposed trip was almost heaven-sent in that it addressed my current mood – to say nothing of fulfilling a life-long ambition. All the factors needed for me to go had come together to make it possible. I might never get another chance as good as this. I agreed with her but when I almost casually formally responded to Nawal and agreed to go I had no idea just how difficult and time-consuming a task lay in front of me.

One of my biggest concerns about the trip had little to do with the difficult terrain, climate or other dangers that we might face. As we were to be a solo car then the two of us were likely to be together, in sometimes very trying circumstances, for 24 hours a day for many weeks. I was not convinced I could survive that experience if it was my wife – let alone a complete stranger! Nawal proved to be a fascinating character. In the event the trip turned out to be much more arduous than I had imagined. Frankly if it had not been for Nawal's tenacity, determination and sheer pig-headedness, then I doubt we could have completed the trip. The whole trip was a fabulous and most intense series of experiences for me. I am not sure that I could ever become a bosom pal of Nawal's as we are very different in too many ways but I shall be forever grateful to him for making this trip happen.

We found that as the trip itself progressed we became increasingly tired. We began to run out of money and the car took a greater and greater hammering. We became uncertain as to whether we would complete the trip and this made the atmosphere tense on occasions. Despite this, or perhaps because of this, we found that whatever our personal differences, we both shared that determined priority to get to Beijing, whatever it took. The recognition of that fact and the realisation that we both needed each other overcame the many minor irritations we had along the way.

In fact, given that we were cocooned together for such a long time and had very different natures, I am more surprised by the degree of harmony between us than the few real arguments that we had.

But, that said, I did find Nawal a very single-minded individual and, in my opinion, pretty self-centred, and these, I found, were extremely difficult characteristics to live with. But on the other hand these were useful traits on an adventure like this. He was bossy. He constantly gave the impression that he felt it was his trip and that as he had invited me along then there was no call to discuss events when a decision had to be reached. After all, he would think, we were going in his car so he called the tune. On top of that I know that he saw me as a typical pampered Englishman. I lived a very comfortable life in a pleasant part of the country. I had earned a very good living and didn't really understand that the rest of the world had to struggle from time to time. He was there to teach me a few things about the world. He also thought it was his duty to ensure that I undertook many menial tasks. Naturally I felt I should play my part in everything that needed to be done but Nawal took it a stage further. He very much considered that he was in charge all along and that this rather soft and spoilt companion of his should be taught what life was like for the masses and therefore be given constant instruction on, for example, the menial tasks relating to the cleaning of the car.

In many respects he had a point. Indeed, I did find that I learned a number of things from him.

I found his philosophy on life fascinating. For example on one occasion I was getting increasingly nervous about the danger of highway robbery as we were travelling through Siberia. He said that I should get a grip on myself (which was true) and that I should try and imagine the worst that might happen. Once I had learnt to accept this then whatever happened thereafter would be no worse and I could therefore cope with it. On first hearing this it seemed to make sense. Some deeply held Moslem or Hindu belief no doubt (I never did ask whether he was a Moslem or a Hindu or neither). I began to think of the practical application of this philosophy. I got to thinking that the worst that could happen was that I could be shot by a bandit and the more I thought about this the less I liked it! I felt that I couldn't just calmly accept that possibility. When I said that I was having difficulty accepting that I might be killed he simply told me to shut up. Which was probably the right thing for him to say anyway but it did nothing to reduce my concern about the dangers ahead. Nor, indeed, for my greater understanding of karma – the Indian 'destiny'.

I also recall three points that he made repeatedly although not often simultaneously. The first was that all material things in life should be shared equally throughout the population. This seemed reasonable on the face of it: each as to his wants regardless of original ownership. The second point was that although he had a good job he didn't have much spare cash. The third point that cropped up repeatedly was that obviously I had led a charmed life and must be very rich to be able to retire early. It was therefore quite clear where he was coming from when it came to discussions as to how we should split the costs between us for any unforeseen expenses etc!

On the other hand I genuinely found him a fascinating character. He talked a bit about racial prejudice and the difficulties this had presented him with from time to time. It is true that I had never really thought about this aspect of life very seriously before. I am sure that he found it difficult, as an intelligent and rather well-to-do Indian, arriving in England about eight years previously and being treated like a pariah. He cited occasions where he felt he had been held back in his promotion prospects at work purely, he felt, because of his race.

I have no doubt that he was an excellent salesman and I saw his tactics in action many a time. He was able to talk the hind legs off a donkey. I think that if he wasn't able to beat the listener into submission then, after hours of conversation, his strategy was to be very selective in repeating what had already been said. For example, when in Moscow, we had been trying to get our sponsors Cadbury's to chip in more money. I was present during a very lengthy conversation between Nawal and the local Cadbury boss, Peter Kirby. Peter repeatedly said that they had already committed sufficient to the cause and were unable to add more. However, at one point, he had said that of course Cadbury's were always willing to look at sponsoring new proposals. It was the first dozen statements of refusal that Nawal completely ignored and he latched on to the remark that Peter was prepared to look at new proposals. Well, weren't we making a new proposal – after all, our plans had changed slightly due to extra demands for payment at the Chinese border? Surely, on the basis of what Peter had already stated, Cadbury's would be sympathetic to this new situation and cough up a little more to help us out? In the end they did. Nawal was nothing if not persistent!

The relationship between two people on a trip such as this would make a fascinating study in itself. As the trip progressed and the various challenges kept coming at us with increasing rapidity, we instinctively knew how the other was likely to react. I found myself becoming calmer and calmer as the trip went on, which was, frankly, quite out of character. Nawal was quite placid most of the time and he was particularly effective when we had problems crossing the Chinese border. On the other hand Nawal certainly had his moments and did flare up occasionally – the more so the further we travelled, it seemed. For example he had a blazing row in China with our 'hosts' when it appeared that they were not taking our request for arranging a couple of days' sightseeing very seriously. I knew that it would be best to prise him away from the Chinese for a while at that moment until he had calmed down a bit. This, coupled with a little bit of extra diplomacy, managed to get us our way. Throughout the trip there were many instances when each of us needed the other. In that sense it was a very successful partnership which worked both ways.

Of course, on first meeting Nawal I did not really know him. It was not until we had spent many weeks together that I began to understand him and know what made him tick. I found him infuriating at times (quite a lot of times, come to think of it!). On the other hand he was tenacious, diplomatic, determined and, fortunately, had a good sense of humour. The journey presented many obstacles and there are very few people who would have been able to patiently overcome them all – Nawal was such a person and I shall be eternally grateful to him for being primarily responsible for ensuring the completion of the most exciting adventure of my life.

3

Preparation

After my meeting with Nawal in January, planning began in earnest. I was still working full-time but had already arranged a departure date from my firm of 31 March. Through February and March I was fortunate in not being expected to play a full role in office life. That was perhaps just as well as I found that the availability of secretaries, phones, fax machines and photocopiers assisted tremendously in the planning stage. There was a great deal to do.

One thing that I found satisfying about the trip was how much I was able to achieve by my own efforts. I had enjoyed a successful career in the City. Don't get me wrong – I was no more successful than many thousands of others, and a great deal less successful than quite a number of well-known names. But I had not noticed that during the past decade or two I had become increasingly reliant on a whole array of individuals and systems that made up my 'infrastructure'. I slowly realised that I had gradually and subconsciously become dependent on it. For example, years ago I had been able to repair my first car whenever it broke down. This was caused by the necessity of having to do so as neither I, nor my friends at the time, had sufficient funds to hire a mechanic. Of course, cars were simpler in those days. My first car was an Austin 10, bought in 1965 for £15 and sold for £25 a year later – my first profitable deal. The engine was simplicity itself and there was plenty of room under the bonnet to complete a 'decoke' with ease. As I progressed to company cars I found my time occupied by other matters. I lost interest in the mechanics and, anyway, the cars themselves became increasingly sophisticated. I wouldn't have

14

been able to repair my company car even if I had wanted to. Although the Austin Healey was a very simple 1960s car, I had forgotten, over the years, all that I had once known.

In a similar vein, as a student, I had been used to organising all my own trips. Although I had subsequently travelled for business reasons to increasingly distant and interesting locations, I had relied more and more on my secretary and in-house travel department. I may have been to exotic spots such as Brunei, Cambodia and Yemen, or even the more obvious ones such as Paris, Frankfurt and New York. However, it was one thing to press a button on the desk and ask my secretary to get me on the next plane to Timbuktu and to make sure she made a reservation in a decent hotel. It was quite another thing to organise a trip myself. I had grown out of the habit. At first I became overwhelmed as I realised the immense task I had let myself in for on this particular trip. But as time went by and each little piece of the large jigsaw began to fit into place I got a real sense of personal achievement and satisfaction. OK, so during the week it took me to get visas for Belarus, for example, my colleagues at work would, quite literally, have turned over millions of pounds' worth of high-powered deals. But the point was that I was beginning to solve every aspect of my own problems, however mundane, for the first time in perhaps 25 years. It was an unusual and very satisfying feeling!

Our biggest challenge was caused by the fact that nobody had ever completed this route before. As I began to cast around for those who could give advice it slowly dawned on me that this was the case. Plenty of people had been to Moscow but few had driven there. Quite a few people had been to Beijing but *nobody* had driven there! One or two people had been to places in between these extremes but most had simply flown directly into, say, Novosibirsk, and then flown out again. A friend of mine – my near neighbour John Oakley – had been on the Trans-Siberian Express, but

15

his comments and descriptions, although interesting, were of limited use to us as drivers.

I suppose that the workload for the preparatory stage was split fairly naturally and evenly between Nawal and me. He looked after the preparation of the car and the relationship with our sponsors. I planned the route, arranged accommodation and petrol supplies where possible, the currency notes required and, indeed, all other items that we needed to take with us given the severely limited space available. We both played a part in raising money for our chosen charity.

Nawal had already been in touch with Children in Crisis, a charity based in London which supports various projects both in this country and abroad. As the name might suggest, their mission is 'to provide help or relief in the case of hardship, distress, sickness or poverty to children in any part of the world irrespective of race, religion or politics to restore hope and dignity'. They have links with the charity Children of Chernobyl based in Minsk and they have a project, namely a rest home for children with health problems, in Poland. They were also aiming, at the time of our departure, to establish a new orphanage in China. As these were all regions through which we hoped to travel and as we both felt that help for the underprivileged of the younger generation was a worthy cause, it seemed to make sense for us to select them as our 'beneficiaries'. In addition to that they were run by very nice people who were keen to assist us in our preparations and showed a general enthusiasm for our project.

In my view, the fact that we were using the trip to raise money for charity was not entirely altruistic. A trip of this magnitude is expensive. We needed at least one major sponsor and serious sponsors would not be attracted unless they judged that they would be seen to be supporting a worthy cause. We thought of a variety of ways in which we could raise money and attended a number of events organised by the CIC charity itself. In the end Nawal organised a local raffle, which raised about £200 and managed to elicit a decent-sized cheque from his employers. I am afraid that I exploited my retirement after 30 years in the City by writing directly to everyone I could think of. Nearly all were extremely generous and I raised about £8,000 from a total of 50 different sources. In the end our total achievement to the charity was comfortably into five figures. But it is a sobering reflection that this was only a fraction of the cost of the trip itself. As anybody who is involved with charity work will know, it is very time-consuming and hard work to raise funds.

We tried to publicise our trip as widely as possible. This would be useful in itself for our chosen charity by raising awareness of their existence and aims. Hopefully, it might also lead to the raising of more funds for them. We were pretty successful on the local scene, with several papers and radio stations giving us numerous plugs. As far as the nationals were concerned, I did manage to get myself mentioned in the *Daily Telegraph*. However, I suspect that this was more to do with my leaving the City to do something unusual (it appeared in their regular 'Men and Matters' section on the City page). I'm sure that several attempts are made each year to embark upon some hare-brained scheme or other and many fail, and the newspapers need greater certainty of at least some success before they run the story. Certainly we found that, even by the time we got to Warsaw, we were receiving a number of enquiries from the British media. These included Reuters and BBC Radio 5, who both gave us coverage at that stage and later.

We had very little time to organise events, given the numerous other matters that needed to be arranged before our departure. I therefore took the view that, as far as raising funds for charity was concerned, the direct plea was the most effective route in the circumstances, and I believe this proved to be the case.

Discussions with our main sponsors were lengthy. Cadbury's had sponsored Nawal on his earlier trip to Moscow so they were a natural first port of call. This worked. Their international corporate structure is one of separate entities in each country. Cadbury's UK were not interested. However we did come across a very friendly individual, Chris Capstick, who operated out of their head offices in Bournville near Birmingham. Although he was unable to acquire any sponsorship money from the UK operation he did act as a useful middleman between the various overseas offices. For example, he pushed the Moscow office into issuing a letter of introduction which was necessary for obtaining a Russian visa. This was after several weeks of pestering from us, and Chris's intervention saved the day in the nick of time. Later, when the trip itself was under way, he proved a useful point of contact and relayed our intermittent messages to various members of the press and to our own 'better halves'.

However, our main contact with our sponsors was with each independent overseas subsidiary. This was Cadbury's Poland based in Warsaw, Cadbury's Russia based in Moscow and Cadbury's China based in. . .would you believe it?. . . Melbourne, Australia! In addition to that we were speaking to a Cadbury's distribution agent in Belarus called Feneron Trading. With each of these entities we were offered a different deal and different things were expected from us. For example some were prepared to give us a fixed cash amount, whereas others would propose paying for, say, petrol and accommodation whilst in their territory. Conversely, one would simply require us to attend a single press conference, whereas another would expect us to park in front of their flagship retail store all day giving away chocolate bars. Nawal's negotiating experience came to the fore at this time and I was very grateful for his skills in this respect. I was also grateful that he was the one to take the many calls from Australia or Moscow in the middle of the night!

Nawal's other major role at this time was to mastermind the preparation of the car. We had decided to have it stripped down and rebuilt with all suspect parts replaced. In the event it was proved that some suspect parts still remained, but we did not know that at the time. This was a very expensive operation and absorbed the bulk of the funds received from our sponsors. The specialist firm of Brown & Gammon in Hertfordshire carried it out. We needed to take a decision on a number of points relating to the car but we had to bear in mind that we were operating on a tight budget. We decided to strengthen the front suspension as this is known to be a weak point on a Healey. We later wished somebody had told us that the rear suspension could also do with strengthening as we found this out to our cost when in the middle of a Siberian forest! We decided to bolt on a skid shield under the engine and a sump guard further back. This was one of our better decisions and undoubtedly saved us from the complete disintegration of the car on the increasingly rough Siberian and Chinese roads. We added halogen spotlamps and also a cigar lighter. We didn't envisage smoking too many Havanas during our odyssey – this was simply to provide a power point to drive a compressor or any other electrically propelled unit. We added bonnet and boot straps for extra security and also fitted an immobiliser. This last decision proved to be a major mistake as we were unable to shut it down when trying to restart the car after a petrol stop in Omsk. It took three precious hours to drill it out!

We also decided to take the hard top for security reasons. This proved sensible. We were concerned that the car might be tampered with if left out overnight or otherwise unattended and a soft top is a positive invitation to an opportunist with a knife. We also felt that a hard top would, to some extent, compensate for the lack of a roll bar should we turn the car over – which we did on one occasion! Unfortunately the hard top option did have its drawbacks. I have driven many Austin Healeys in my time and have found that the heater unit operates in exactly the same way in each car. Whatever the setting, in either winter or summer, absolutely nothing happens for the first 5 miles and then heat is blasted out like a furnace, especially on the passenger side. Much of our journey was in hot weather and the hard top acted to convert the Healey into a mobile sauna. The only beneficial aspect was that I managed to sweat away more than a stone and a half of my middle-age spread during our transcontinental trip.

We had to bear in mind that we did not want to alter the car too much from its original state. We decided against the purchase of a 'straightened' boot lid, which would have doubled the volume inside the boot and, our biggest mistake by far, decided against fitting a rally exhaust system. The ground clearance of the vehicle was a big problem being only 4⅝ inches when unladen. The exhaust pipe, running the whole length of the car, was the lowest point. It was extremely vulnerable to knocks and was difficult to protect. In fact this, although by no means our most serious mechanical problem, was by far our most regular problem and accounted, cumulatively, for several days' delay. We calculated that we had to stop to repair the exhaust on no less than 30 occasions! Sometimes this would be a half-hour stop to re-tighten a jubilee clip, at other times a half or even full day in what passed as a garage as we re-welded certain joints. If we had had the foresight and fitted a rally exhaust from the outset then we would have avoided these problems because this would have been attached directly to the manifold and come straight out of the side of the bonnet. This would have totally avoided the need for a pipe to run underneath the length of the car. Ah well – it's easy to be wise after the event.

It was my job to try to obtain visas for those countries requiring them, namely: Belarus, Russia and China – although the obtaining of the Chinese visa was a story in itself and was, in the event, left to the Beijing office of Cadbury's to sort out. My first port of call was the Belarus embassy, where I was introduced straight away to the very affable consul, Mr Yakovitski. He explained that there is normally a charge for such a service but that as we were essentially on a charity run he would be happy to waive this charge. I was to leave the passports and call back next week. He was good to his promise; I found the passports ready for me on my return and they now included a very impressive multicoloured Belarussian stamp. Mr Yakovitski also supplied me with a note on headed embassy paper in English and Russian briefly describing the nature of our trip and requesting all concerned to avoid any let or hindrance to our safe and swift passage. I just hoped that any bandits would (a) be able to speak Russian and (b) respect the authority of the Belarus London embassy – some hope, but a crumb of comfort is better than no comfort at all, I felt!

Furthermore the consul offered to drive me personally to the Russian embassy, just across the way in Knightsbridge, to help facilitate my request for a Russian visa. I was expecting a Rolls Royce with outriders or, at the very least, a smart Jaguar car so I was a little less impressed when we both squeezed into a small and ancient Lada. Nevertheless I was extremely grateful for his assistance throughout and it was in marked contrast to the reaction I got from the Russian officials.

By the time we arrived at the Russian embassy gates they had closed for the day so I was left to my own devices to call back the next day. I took note that the opening times for the visa office were 8 a.m. until 3 p.m. for each weekday except Wednesdays. I thought I would give the embassy staff a little time to organise themselves, so I turned up the next day at 8.30 a.m. and found myself confronted by a queue which must have been a good 100 yards long. It perhaps didn't help that the newspapers that very morning were full of a tit-for-tat spy story. The Brits had expelled 20 Russians from London and the Russians had immediately retaliated by expelling the same number of British officials from Moscow. Whether that had temporarily soured relationships to such a point that obtaining a visa was made more difficult, or whether the Russians were always plain awkward in these matters, I shall never know. I do know that obtaining a Russian visa proved a nightmare. After waiting in the queue for four hours, it became apparent that the Russians allowed people into the embassy in batches of about a dozen at a time. However, they never announced when this process had ceased. There would normally be a little shuffle of the queue every half-hour or so but when this did not happen for over an hour the rumour went around that they had closed for the day. Nobody from the embassy went to the simple trouble of posting a notice to this effect on the gate or informing us in any other way. But it was true – the embassy had closed for visas for the day even though it was earlier than the posted time. This was all good experience for the sort of bureaucratic frustrations that we later encountered in Russia itself and which the long-suffering Russian people have had to accept as a matter of daily routine. I had moved from being 100 yards from the gates to perhaps 80 yards and that had been the sole achievement of the day!

The next day I thought I would phone the embassy and organise a visa by phone, leaving me the task of collection only. However, I could, at first, only get through to an answering machine which gave the times that the embassy was open. Through directory enquiries I discovered another number but as soon as I mentioned that I was looking for a visa they simply put the phone down.

More determined than ever, I set out extremely early the next morning and arrived at the embassy at the uncivilised hour of 7 a.m. The advantage at that hour, I discovered, was that the queue was a mere 80 yards long. However, with the very slow process that the Russian system engendered and with total lack of any information from embassy staff to explain the chances for anyone in the queue, I stuck it out until 2 p.m. At that time, despite the official closure time of 3 p.m., the shutters again came down. The rumour circulated that the gates were closed and with no further queue shuffles to indicate another lucky dozen had got through, we all decided that this must indeed be the case so we all set off to go home again. How Russians themselves can be so stoic and uncomplaining about this totally inefficient organisation I have no idea. I cannot understand, either, the logic of the embassy staff. Surely it would be helpful to their economy or, if nothing else, to the financing of the London embassy, if they were to encourage as many big-spending westerners as possible. Why don't they make visa acquisition easy – or even possible?

My problem was now becoming pressing because we had suffered delays from Cadbury's in Moscow. They had promised to send an official letter of invitation, which was a necessary accompaniment for a visa application. But after several weeks of constant requests and reminders from us we did not receive the letter of invitation until just two weeks before our departure date. I had already spent one week of this time in my fruitless queuing. However, on my last visit I had got close enough to the head of the queue to notice that a number of individuals appeared to be entering via a separate gateway. Clutching several passports at a time, they were entering the embassy a good half-hour before the stated opening times. These turned out to be the couriers, who all seemed to be freelance operators. I spoke to them and was put in touch with a burly character named Con who came from Walthamstow. He said he had been dealing with 'the Ruskies' for 20 years and they were 'a decent bunch really'. If I left the passports with him then I could call round at his flat in Walthamstow four working days later to collect them. He asked for 'fifty quid in bunce' for his troubles plus another £120 for the visas. The Russians had a sliding scale of charges and we had left it to the last minute which, naturally, was the most expensive. I felt a little uncertain giving my new-found shady-looking friend £170 in cash, but what was more disconcerting was releasing the passports. How could we possibly get the trip under way if we never saw them, or Con, again, given the short time we had left? I was beginning to wonder if the name 'Con' was an omen. I made a couple of quick enquiries from a pair of equally shady-looking characters who were lurking under a nearby tree. They both said that Con was 'a good bloke'. So with no further ado I gave Con the cash and passports and waved goodbye.

True to his word, when I appeared at his somewhat obscure high-rise flat in Walthamstow a few days later, there was Con plus passports and visas. Another problem solved. But I never did dare tell Nawal that with just one week to go I had given the passports to a complete stranger for a few days.

We were trying to conclude the initial planning for all aspects of our trip simultaneously. Around this time we also encountered problems obtaining the Chinese visas. I would have thought it a simple process. I had telephoned the Chinese embassy in London and explained that we were driving across the Chinese border and would therefore require the necessary forms to obtain the requisite visas. They said, 'Sir, I have to inform you that there is a law in China stating that no foreigner is permitted to drive a car. Therefore there is no such thing as a visa for a car – I am sorry.' They then put the phone down. I didn't know how true this statement was so I relayed the problem to Cadbury's office in Beijing (via Melbourne!) and the eventual reply was that they would hope to sort it out in Beijing. In the event this was still one of the remaining unresolved issues at our time of departure from the UK, but more of that later.

The route itself was fairly simple to plan. We needed to call at Warsaw, Minsk, Moscow and Beijing in order to visit each of our sponsors and conduct some promotional work for them. That being the case there was very little choice of route. It was simply a matter of travelling east to Moscow, then further east across the southern part of Siberia, skirting Outer Mongolia to our immediate south. Once past Outer Mongolia, we would turn due south to cross into China at the first crossing point at Zabaykalsk in Russia to Manzhouli in the Inner Mongolian region of northern China. Cadbury's China wanted us to do some promotional work in about half a dozen cities in China so this meant travelling in a sweeping arc down to Beijing in order to pass through cities such as Qiqihar, Harbin, Changchun and Shenyang. I had barely heard of most of these cities, which says a lot about the ignorance of the typical westerner, or me at any rate, when one considers that these are all major

24

communities, each with populations running into several million.

Of course it was one thing drawing a line on a map, it was quite another confirming whether a road existed or not! We phoned the Russian embassy again – this time a different section. We explained our mission and enquired about petrol supplies and road conditions. They had no comment on petrol availability. They said that the roads to Moscow were OK and 'probably' all right thereafter as far as Irkutsk but they weren't too sure about this. They had never heard of anyone driving further than Moscow. They had heard that there was no road from Irkutsk, 'only a direction'. We laughed at what we thought was a joke but, on the journey itself, as we travelled further and further east, we heard this comment on several occasions from a variety of different people and, indeed, it turned out to be pretty accurate.

I don't know if you have ever bought a map of Russia. The one in my local bookshop is typical. There is a lot of detail on the one side that shows European Russia up to Moscow and slightly beyond. Turn over to the other side and the scale changes, quite literally, to 15 million to one. There is a huge green blob representing Siberia, with a very thin spidery line crossing it as far as the Pacific coastline at Vladivostok. This turns out to be the Trans-Siberian Railway. There are a lot of rivers and forests but very little else. Not much shown in the way of roads. I went to my favourite map shop, Stanfords in Covent Garden, and unearthed a road map of Siberia which was produced some years ago by the American air force. Rather disconcertingly there was a second map also produced by the American air force which showed quite a different set of roads. By this time we had discovered two travel firms who had a bit of knowledge of this part of the world and were very helpful. But, again, this was only up to a point.

When we started out with the whole idea we had thought that, if we completed the trip, we might be the first classic car to complete it unaided. As time went on we began to realise that we might be the first vehicle of any description to complete this direct route from London to Beijing and we are now as sure as we can be that this was the case. Inevitably, therefore, there were no 'experts' who could give us an answer to all our questions. Hence my earlier reference to a jigsaw puzzle which was solved painstakingly bit by bit.

Our two travel companies were the well-known Lonely Planet company and the perhaps less well-known but fascinating Exodus travel company based in south London. I went down to see these Exodus characters and had lunch with them. They organise a number of unusual holidays to various places in the world. In the case of Russia at that time, they flew people into places like Krasnoyarsk or Irkutsk and then took them around in a purpose-built vehicle to explore the surrounding countryside. Of course this was very different to what we were proposing to do. They had safety in numbers, were pretty self-sufficient in petrol and food as they had plenty of storage space and, of course, were only exploring one particular region. Nevertheless their comments were useful. We were encouraged that they were fairly sure that there was some sort of road system all the way across. We also knew that although the Sino-Soviet border was still perhaps one of the most heavily guarded in the world and had been a flashpoint only a couple of years earlier, they felt that an increasing number of Chinese traders were beginning to use this crossing point. And that is what we, also, chose to believe at the time!

I began to realise that in a venture such as this there was only so far one could go in the preparation. In my business life I had been used to ensuring that all eventualities were catered for wherever possible and that there was always a contingency plan if things went wrong somewhere along the line. In this case, however, there was nobody who actually knew what the true situation was. Nobody could confirm that we would have adequate food or petrol supplies nor that we would find secure accommodation at night nor that the roads would be passable. We got to the point, therefore, whereby we had a choice of either abandoning the whole idea or just trusting to luck and going anyway. We chose the latter.

We knew that we were to spend a few days in Warsaw as the guests of the local Cadbury company. This somewhat dictated our cross-Channel route as it strongly attracted us to try for the overnight ferry from Harwich to the Hook of Holland. This would allow us a good night's sleep on board and we could commence our trans-European segment at an early hour. The alternative of the short crossing to France would mean many extra miles driving and an additional stopover before Warsaw. We hoped we could make Poland on our first day in continental Europe, and in the event we did. Stena Lines operated the only ferry on this route. I had written to most cross-Channel ferry companies by this time and had received a promise of a free crossing from two of them in return for some publicity, but from Stena Line I got a standard reply that 'due to the large number of requests we receive we regret that we are unable . . .' It was exactly the same wording that I had used on many occasions when turning down charity requests addressed to my firm. I was now at the receiving end for a change and vowed that if I ever again became a charity officer of some firm I would change the wording as it was obviously too standardised and somewhat cold. But at least I got a reply. However, this really was the ferry we needed and I persisted. I was eventually put in touch directly with a Mr Lanning who turned out to be very sympathetic to our quest. He, naturally, required some proof of the charitable nature of our venture but, subject to that, was prepared to offer us free passage. This was only for the one direction, of course, as on the return leg we planned to fly back after arranging for the car to be containerised and then shipped from a Chinese port to Harwich or Felixstowe.

There was a mass of other decisions that needed to be taken and an amazing amount of work still to be completed before we were ready. Time was racing by. We aimed to depart in mid-May, as this was perhaps the best time of year, climatically, to pass through Siberia. Of course the whole subject of climatic conditions was another uncertainty for us. We asked our two expert and experienced travel companies what we were likely to encounter in this respect so that we might best prepare ourselves. It was amusing that we received a written reply from each of them on the same day. Lonely Planet told us that our biggest problem would be the ice and snow that we would encounter through the mountain sections. This could be quite severe even in summer and therefore we ought to consider thoroughly lagging the car (and ourselves). By contrast, Exodus travel said that our biggest problem would be the severe heat. We had to remember that we would be travelling in high summer across the biggest land mass on earth. The heat would bring with it attendant problems of dust. We had better prepare ourselves for this heat and ensure we had efficient filters for the car (air, oil etc.) with numerous spares in order to combat the dusty conditions. In the event we opted for the latter point of view which, indeed, proved to be the more accurate.

There were plenty of other details that took a lot of time and effort to resolve. For example, we decided that we would display Russian and Chinese characters on the side of the car which would briefly explain our mission. Not only would this be helpful for the population who saw us pass by but, we hoped, might just swing the difference if stopped by aggressive policemen if we had transgressed some minor traffic offence or, worse, were accosted by bandits. On reflection, I suspect that it would have taken a bit more than a notice to prevent a hardened armed robber but I suppose that we worked on the theory that a little bit of comfort is better than none at all. However, my local signwriter, understandably, didn't have a clue as to how to create an adequate slogan in either Russian or Chinese. It took a lot of time and several faxes back and forth to Moscow and Beijing before we managed to get a template organised.

We had to decide what to pack. The Austin Healey is a very simple car. It has a big 3-litre engine, a couple of seats and a steering wheel and not much else. There certainly wasn't much thought given at the design stage to a requirement for extensive luggage space. The boot is tiny. In our case it was completely filled with spares (mainly electrical) and tools. We had a boot rack which took three spare tyres, a rug and a jerrycan. We decided against a roof rack for security reasons and, after a little bit of thought, against towing a trailer. In the space behind the seats we packed:

- two sleeping bags
- maps and navigation equipment plus guidebooks and phrase books for several countries
- first-aid kit
- thermos flasks
- water purifier
- fire extinguisher
- petrol cans
- spare oil cans
- torch
- petrol enhancer
- passports, documents and letters
- cameras – one 35mm, one video, one Polaroid.

That left us just the tiny door pockets for all our personal effects including wash bag and all clothes. I must say that now more than ever I truly believe in the old adage: 'When you pack for a trip, take half the amount of clothes that you think you will require and double the amount of money and you'll probably be about right'. As far as clothes were concerned, we travelled very lightly, with one spare pair of everything but nothing else: literally two pairs of socks, two pairs of shoes, two pairs of pants (actually I sneaked in a third!), two pairs of shorts, two trousers, two T-shirts, one jumper, one waterproof jacket. That was it and it was perfectly adequate for the whole of the seven weeks. Mind you, I suppose I was lucky in that I have a very weak sense of smell!

I think a further word on the equipment that we carried would be useful. We had decided to try to reach a major city each night and, when planning the route, I thought this would be possible despite the long distances between centres of civilisation (a relatively loose term when applied to Siberia) the further east we went. I had guessed that a distance of about 300 miles a day was about right for the conditions we were likely to encounter. We needed to estimate our timings reasonably accurately in order to commit ourselves to making the various meetings and press conferences that had been planned for us. According to the map, this sort of daily distance should also allow us to reach a populated area each night, although on some of the eastern Siberian sections this would have to be stretched a bit more. In the event there were several occasions where it had to be stretched a lot more! I thought this would take us about seven hours of travelling per day plus stops. I think I proved to be about right as far as the daily average distance was concerned but often hopelessly inaccurate as to the time it would take. On one day in northern China we travelled 22 hours non-stop apart from a brief petrol pick-up, against what I thought was our conservative expectation that that leg would take just six hours! The idea of reaching a major city was that both the car and we were more likely to be secure, particularly if we could find an hotel with a lock-up garage facility. For that reason the sleeping bags were only for 'emergency' use in the event that we might find ourselves stranded in a forest.

The maps, guides and other documents were, together, quite bulky although we later jettisoned some as we moved into China. We took Lonely Planet guidebooks for Poland, Russia and China. We found them invaluable. We also took a Berlitz phrase book for each of these three countries and a series of pencils and pens and a small compass. Our maps took up quite a bit of room as we took eight detailed ones covering Siberia, as well as two for China and just one for the whole of Europe including Moscow. The documents included our passports and visas and a number of letters written on behalf of the charity, the Belarus consul and others, in a variety of languages, which we hoped would help in any potentially difficult situation.

We were advised to take US dollars with us in cash. These were to be in small notes with no imperfections and all dated post 1992. We took $3,000 in bundles of ones, fives, tens and twenties. These we stuck under the carpet, behind the seats, in the boot – anywhere in fact just to disperse them. I worked on the theory that if one bunch was lost or stolen then we would at least have some others left. Our problems with this system were threefold. Firstly a thunderstorm when crossing Germany, given the leaky nature of an Austin Healey, meant that most notes were thoroughly soaked and unusable for some considerable time. Secondly we forgot where we put them all and, given the very tightly packed nature of our luggage soon found that it took a long time to unearth the next bundle when required. The third and most surprising aspect, particularly for me as an ex-foreign exchange dealer, was that once we had got as far as about a thousand miles east of Moscow we found the population increasingly conservative. Despite the fragile state of the Russian ruble on the world's financial markets, they would accept nothing but their own currency. This was in marked contrast to the shrewder and more 'streetwise' population and institutions in Moscow earlier who would *only* accept US dollars and wouldn't touch their own currency with a bargepole!

We also brought a Global Positioning System with us. This GPS machine is quite an incredible instrument as it can pinpoint any position in the world to within 20 yards by obtaining a fix on a minimum of 3 of the 24 satellites circling the earth for this purpose. It is quite small, indeed is hand-held, being little larger than a pocket calculator. It can also calculate other statistics, such as our relative speed and our compass bearing to the next target. It was an invention of the US military but is now widely and relatively cheaply available anywhere. It was fascinating to use – even though we never managed to wire it up correctly and therefore managed to get through hundreds of batteries as we were unable to use direct current from the car. Having said that, I initially thought that it would be more of a gimmick in our case and only of limited practical use. Although I had a bit of fun using it, I still believe that this was the case and it was, therefore, an unnecessary expense and luxury. It would have made more sense in a boat, where one could travel in any horizontal direction. Even more so in an aeroplane or hot-air balloon where one had the added alternative of a choice of altitude. But faced with a T-junction in the road it was little help to know that our objective was straight ahead, for example. The only times we got lost were when we were driving through a major city. What we really needed was a street map and a good command of either Russian or Chinese – unfortunately we had neither and the GPS system was of no benefit in those situations.

It was difficult to decide on the contents of the first-aid kit. It was possible to argue that we might need everything that was available from the chemist's shop (or hospital) as anything could happen. But again we were very limited for space. We took sterilised hypodermic needles just in case, some Elastoplast, bandages, insect repellent, aspirin, salt tablets and Imodium. The only item we used was the Elastoplast. We had a rule that no one was allowed to bleed in the car. If we were cut, which did frequently happen given the amount of running repairs that we undertook, we had to wrap the wound in a cloth until the bleeding had stopped and then use an Elastoplast. I think the only bodily accident that I can recall other than minor cuts was when I burnt my forearm on the exhaust pipe. This gave me quite a 'war wound', which I took great delight in showing off when I got home, but, sadly, it eventually wore off.

I think it's worth making another point on the subject of health. I am the sort of person that gets a queasy tummy on a weekend trip to Spain. I can honestly say that in the whole of our seven-week trip I never felt the slightest bit ill in any respect. That is all the more surprising when you consider what we ate, assuming it could always be identified, and the prolonged periods when we didn't eat at all. I put this rare burst of perfect health down to two factors. The first was the invaluable water purifier. This was Nawal's idea in the first place and proved well worthwhile. As he said, most poison absorbed on intake comes from the liquids not the solids. We should only drink boiled water as in tea etc. or ensure everything was purified – even potable water from hotel taps. The second aspect was that even though I spent most of my time in the passenger seat rather than the driver's seat there was always an incredible amount to do. On top of which the adrenaline was constantly flowing. We felt we were always a hair's breadth away from another breakdown or a possible crash. There were always problems with officials such as the regular police patrols. There was the growing feeling, as we continued and the car took more and more damage, that we might well not make it. And yet the further we managed to get, the more determined we became to complete the whole trip. This constant state of hype never allowed me to relax and consider whether I had a headache or stomach-ache. It took my mind off these matters as I was forced to concentrate all the time on the job in hand.

The thermos flasks were useful. Often we could get little in the way of food in the mornings, even if we were staying at a hotel; perhaps a stale roll. However, we could always get hot water, from which we could make tea. We found this a truly refreshing drink as we went along. Sadly, both thermos flasks broke before we had even left Russia.

Luckily we never needed the fire extinguisher.

Nawal was a good photographer and brought along his high-quality camera with a wide range of filters and lenses. This took up quite a bit of precious room, in fact all that was available between the front seats. However, it was well worth it. I was the video cameraman and again, although much of the resultant video was taken from behind the windscreen as we drove along, it was well worth the effort as we now have an excellent record of events in two media. I took about eight hours of video altogether but have edited the highlights to a single tape of two hours. At the time we really didn't give too much thought to taking photographs because there was so much else to do. This applied particularly to the major incidents during the trip. The last thing we thought of when we had a problem was to get out and take photographs. It was all hands to the pump in order to get us safely on our way again. How I envied Michael Palin, who managed to have many adventures on his various trips and still had a TV crew to record every highlight. Nevertheless, considering we did not have a professional camera crew following our every move, I believe we have a very good record of most events and, overall, this gives a true feeling of the emotions and feelings we enjoyed (or should I say suffered?) whilst travelling. I took about 80 of Nawal's still photographs and had them made into slides. These have proved an indispensable aid when giving talks about our venture. On this latter point it is quite surprising just how many different groups are keen to get speakers as, altogether, I must have given over 30 talks about this trip just to local groups.

Like most people, I am not an accomplished after-dinner speaker and in my early talks I suppose I was quite nervous. However, as time progressed and I began to realise which format went down the best and which jokes to include and which not to include etc., I even began to enjoy the talks myself. Furthermore, they couldn't all have been too horrendous as I have had several repeat requests. Or perhaps it's just that the dearth of good speakers is more acute than I imagined!

We bought oil in Germany on our way through at enormous expense as a last-minute panic in case it might not be available thereafter. On the question of fuel, we were advised that it was difficult to obtain once we had left Germany. However, our arrangement with our Polish, Belarussian and Chinese sponsors was that they would provide the fuel. Unfortunately, on the very long haul stretch across Russia where it really mattered, we were not so lucky in our arrangements. We were not sure what to expect. Our guidebooks said that 96 octane was only available in the cities and even then coupons would be required. I think this was outdated information because coupons were in fact never required. What we were not sure about was the quality and availability of petrol, particularly on those long stretches in the east. We knew that 76 octane would be available but as we were not driving a tractor or heavy machine that could cope with such low-grade fuel this was of little consequence. It may have been possible to retard the timing to cope with the occasional fill-up, but this could not go on indefinitely and would in any event play havoc with the engine. We took fuel enhancer, which was useful. In the event we managed to avoid 76 octane altogether but sometimes found 90 octane the best available. In those circumstances we simply tipped in a phial of enhancer which seemed to do the trick. We never had any problems resulting from incorrect fuel intake. We didn't know what to expect at the outset though, so we started out carrying extra cans of petrol, which we tied to the boot rack. In the end the extra weight proved a significantly greater problem than the perceived difficulty in finding fuel. But that story comes later.

Suffice to say that at this initial stage we made the best guess we could but, in the absence of firm facts, had to trust to luck that we had made sufficient correct guesses to get us through.

Last-minute hitches to our plans, particularly delays that we suffered on the car rebuild, meant that our proposed departure date was postponed by a day or two on several occasions. Then we got a fax from Warsaw – our first official port of call – to say that they had made arrangements for a press conference on Tuesday, 28 May – just one week away. We knew they couldn't alter the date so it was now or never!

The journey itself seemed to fall into three distinct sections. The first was quite civilised and, although we didn't realise it at the time, by far the easiest. This was the section from the UK to Holland, across the breadth of Germany and Poland, through Warsaw and on into Belarus, where we spent time in Minsk, and finally on to our stop in Moscow. Our various sponsors were relatively close to each other along this section so, with our frequent press conferences and promotional work and some sightseeing, it was a leisurely pace as far as the motoring was concerned.

The second phase was the 4,500 mile slog from Moscow across the Siberian wastes, through increasingly hostile terrain, to the Chinese border. This section did indeed prove to be a serious endurance test both for us and the car, with many incidents en route.

The third part was the crossing of the Sino-Soviet border and being met by a team of Chinese officials who would escort us 1,500 miles through the remote northern regions of Inner Mongolia and on through the increasingly congested urban areas approaching Beijing. Our trip was to culminate in a 'victory drive' round Tiananmen Square. But that was 8,000 miles, 7 weeks and 101 'difficult moments' still ahead of us!

On Sunday afternoon, 26 May, with mixed feelings of trepidation and excitement, we set off. We waved goodbye to a crowd of about 100 well-wishers and drove, uneventfully, from my home in Bishop's Stortford to the night ferry at Harwich. This would take us across to Holland and on, we hoped, eventually . . . to China!

4

Across Europe

After the last few hectic days, despite my uncertainties about the difficulties that we might face in the coming days and weeks, it felt a great relief to be on our way. We were very relaxed during our short drive up to Harwich. We caused quite a stir as we waited in the ferry queue. An Austin Healey, as with almost any other classic car, can cause interest by itself. In our case we had the Chinese and Russian slogans plus the inscription of our names as driver and navigator on the sides of the doors in similar fashion to the true rally drivers. We also had a miniature version of the flags of each country depicted on the bonnet. All this combination of extra colour added to the unusual appearance of our vehicle. Many people came to talk to us and we were delighted that some gave a donation for the charity. Once on board the Stena Line ship, the *Konnigen Beatrix*, we enjoyed what might well have been our last supper. In my case, duck washed down with good claret, followed by hot cherries, cheese, coffee and liqueurs. I think we blew a week's anticipated expenses in one evening. But the point was that we wanted to start in style. We really didn't know what to expect for the next few weeks.

We woke early and, it being a bank holiday Monday on the Continent, the motorways were relatively free of traffic. I have never understood why the opposite is usually the case in the UK. I assume the Continental mind prefers to relax at home or travel short distances to see local friends. In the UK we all seem to take the bank holiday weekend as an opportunity to travel to the other end of the country.

The weather was cool and wet. Even at this early stage of

37

the trip we had a few problems. When attempting a simple motorway exit in Holland, Nawal touched the brakes, with the result that we simply aquaplaned further down the motorway and missed our turn. We learnt our lesson. With the Healey being so overloaded, when pools of water were lying on the road surface we would simply have to travel more slowly. The rain did have the benefit of causing the interior of the car to be cooler than normal. However, it didn't take long for the two of us to be soaked to the skin. A Healey top, even a hard top, only repels the rain to a certain extent. Persistent downpours always have a way, or several ways, of finding the cracks in the roof, windows and door frames.

We made good progress as far as Berlin but then hit heavy traffic which slowed us down considerably. Our route so far had been virtually all on motorway or dual carriageway. We simply wanted to get across Western Europe as quickly as possible and save any spare time that we might have for sightseeing in the more unusual locations further east. We were both relatively familiar with the scenery thus far and, looking through my scrapbook, I see that we took just one photograph of our journey throughout the whole of Holland and Germany. This was of a Dutch windmill, which I think we took simply to prove that we had actually crossed the Netherlands!

When we stopped for fuel on the Berlin outer ring road we discovered that we could get no oil reading from the dipstick. This was puzzling. If we really had lost 7 litres of oil then why was the engine running so smoothly? We thought this fact would discount the split oil ring theory but we couldn't come up with an alternative suggestion. Perhaps the 500 miles of motorway driving that day had heated the engine to such an extent that the oil had been thinned so much that it wouldn't register on the dipstick. This was also somewhat unlikely and we were baffled. Obviously our major concern was that we had several thousand arduous miles still ahead of us and the last thing we wanted was an oil leak before we'd really started.

We purchased 16 litres of fresh oil, paid for by US dollar notes that had been drenched by the earlier thunderstorm. There was a distinct lack of any German humour as the garage proprietor made a pointed gesture of hanging each individual banknote on a peg above a radiator before he would let us go on our way. We discussed the problem as we approached Polish territory. The border was quite easy to negotiate but that was probably because we simply ignored the mile-long double queue of cars and drove up the hard shoulder. At the head of the queue we pleaded a combination of ignorance and our charity mission and it seemed to work. We got through swiftly.

There had been tremendous construction activity throughout eastern Germany in the short time following the collapse of the Berlin wall and the reunification of the country. I had actually driven as far as Berlin before (in a modern BMW) shortly after reunification and the road had been very patchy. Since that time huge armies of workers had made significant improvements and it was only the final 10 miles or so at the other side of Berlin leading to the Polish border that remained in a poor state. The difference in road surface was most marked and I saw it as just one small symbol of the contrast between the huge economic strides that Germany had made in the last 50 years compared to the stagnation, and even decline, of the Soviet system over the same period.

I was aware that Poland was largely an agricultural nation and a poor one at that. The state itself is over 1,000 years old and many of the towns and villages appeared little changed from medieval times. Our first impressions of the country supported that initial description. It was, in many ways, like stepping back several generations. Very basic machinery in the fields and little of interest in the few small villages through which we passed. We lost count of the number of horse-drawn ploughs that we observed in the adjoining fields. The abiding memory I have of this first day in Poland was of rustic calm and quaint houses. Maybe there is something to be said for the easier pace of an earlier age. Mind you, it was one thing to observe the scene from our vantage point – quite another to have to live oneself, or bring up a family, in a land with little in the way of modern creature comforts.

The first town of any size was Swiebodzin, and Cadbury's in Warsaw had reserved rooms for us in a local hotel. The hotel façade suggested basic accommodation but the rooms were actually very good and the dinner we ordered in the rather sombre and small dining area was really excellent, so we had no complaints at all – particularly as our main sponsors were picking up the bill! We went to bed pleased that we had achieved our objective in the first day, having covered 550 miles and crossed one major border. However, we remained concerned about the mystery of the missing oil. We thought we might have to take the cylinder head off the car once we got to Warsaw and this would not only cause delays but would mean, effectively, 'running in' the car all over again. Perhaps if we could have done this in our own time on smooth roads then there would be no problem, but as we were about to embark on the rough terrain of Eastern Europe then it was less than ideal.

We had planned to spend between three and four full days in Poland. This would have meant spending two days in Warsaw then taking a detour south to visit the Children in Crisis haven for youngsters located in the small southern Polish town of Lippa Wielka. We had arranged to spend an afternoon and night with them and then, because we were so close, visit the old concentration camp of Auschwitz the next day. This wasn't exactly something we were looking forward to but we both felt that we just had to do it. Unfortunately though, as we were already having engine problems, this whole detour might have to be omitted. We would instead have to spend at least three days in Warsaw and then continue eastwards in order to catch up with the schedule of events already set up for us in Minsk and Moscow.

On our relatively short journey the next morning from Swiebodzin to Warsaw we suffered the first of our many

40

exhaust problems. Already the roads were bad in patches, particularly through the cities. There appeared to be no bypasses and we therefore had to travel through congested built-up areas. The main problem for us, given our limited ground clearance, were the tramlines in all the major cities, which often jutted out from the road surface by several inches. Although we drove gingerly the inevitable happened and in the middle of the city of Poznan we heard a grating sound underneath the car. We pulled in to the side and discovered that the exhaust pipe had broken its rear restraining clip and was dragging on the road. We tied it up to the rear bumper with thick wire.

We hadn't even reached our first major contact point in Warsaw let alone made any serious inroads into our 8,000-mile trek. Imagine how I felt as we limped into Warsaw with our bandaged exhaust and an unknown problem which drained the oil and could cause the engine to seize up at any moment. This state of affairs hardly inspired me with confidence and it was at this point that I first began to have grave doubts about our chances of success. I thought, rather wistfully, of the days when I took just an hour or two to fly in comfort to Eastern Europe. What a contrast!

Anyway, there was little time to dwell on our concerns. As we travelled through the Wielkopolska region (translated as 'Great Poland') heading for Warsaw, I already felt a twinge of excitement. Here we were on just our second day and already we had left the Western Europe that we knew so well and were entering, for us, uncharted territory. Despite the internal excitement that I felt I have to admit that the landscape was flat and uninspiring with just the occasional woodland area to add a bit of interest. Our stoppages, coupled with heavy traffic, had already cut our arrival time in Warsaw pretty fine as we were due to attend a press conference at 3 p.m. We arrived at our hotel, the Europejski, at 2.15 p.m. Members of the PR firm Euro-RSCG greeted us on the steps. I must say that the Polish arm of Cadbury's really had got their act together. They were professional throughout and they milked us for all the

41

publicity they could get, and quite rightly too. The arrivals team immediately rushed us off to the venue for our conference: a beautiful old building in the centre of Warsaw. I subsequently learnt that this was the *only* central Warsaw building of any size to have survived the Second World War. I found that the cliché 'travel broadens the mind' really came true throughout this trip. I have a reasonable sense of history as it was one of my favourite subjects at school but I never realised the full extent of the damage caused by the Second World War to those countries on Germany's eastern front, particularly Russia and Poland. Ninety-five per cent of all Warsaw's buildings were destroyed in the war.

We were asked to make a 'grand entrance' through the gardens of this old mansion and as we emerged through the trees near the front doors we were met with a barrage of photographers. I don't know what Cadbury's had said about us but they really pulled out all the stops and had managed to get several TV crews as well as about 60 journalists to cover this conference. Either they had exaggerated immensely about our mission or else there was very little other news in Poland that day!

As we got out of the car there were loud cheers and we were ushered to the front of the room, where we sat between the MD of Cadbury's Poland and the interpreter. The MD made a speech based on how his company was always keen to support charity work and he noted that we were raising funds for projects in Poland. Then there were a lot of questions asked of us about the trip itself and the logistics. We were there for two hours. After that we were taken straight to the Polish TV station where we gave an interview. This was completed just in time to appear as a feature in the national news broadcast at 7.30 p.m.

We were rushed back to the hotel, where we were given just five minutes to check in, as we had not had time earlier. Then we were driven to a modern restaurant on the out-skirts of the city, where we enjoyed a superb dinner. The service was slow but the surroundings were unusual and our

42

half-dozen young hosts – all members of the PR team – were intelligent, lively and enthusiastic both about our trip and about life in Poland at that time. Given the desperate problems that the Poles have suffered over recent decades because of their geographic position, being squeezed between the two European superpowers of Germany and Russia, then this was an interesting time to be a young Pole. For the first time in several generations Poland was not dominated by either of its large neighbours. There was a sense of freedom and opportunity. The Poles, not just our hosts for the evening but the very many we met elsewhere, were desperate to ensure that Poland was seen as an integral part of Europe. This was their first real chance to break away from the old Soviet influences and they meant to do all in their power to ensure Poland became a strong and independent country. They were a very good bunch of people and we enjoyed our time there immensely. I wished them the best of luck in rebuilding the resources of their country. The conversation over dinner concerned these big issues but as the evening wore on and the wine and then the cocktails flowed, a more relaxed atmosphere pervaded. Feeling very happy, we arrived back at our hotel in the small hours of the morning.

Perhaps thanks to the alcohol, or maybe simply the excellent evening overall, I slept well in my spacious and old-fashioned hotel bedroom. At 7.30 we met for breakfast and were collected a little later by Sanchia Berg, then the BBC's correspondent in Warsaw. She took us to the BBC recording studio in the suburbs. I imagine that this was just what a clandestine broadcasting unit was like in the war. We were taken to a dreary block of high-rise flats in a residential area and then up to the twelfth floor in a creaky, old and smelly lift. After the clanking sound made by the unlocking of the several bolts and other security devices on the grey door of the flat, we went in to discover a mass of dials, buttons, lights and microphones. We were swiftly connected to the Radio 5 studios in London and gave a joint interview. This was to be broadcast at 10.30 that morning London time. Jenny later told me that we were given about ten minutes' airtime and she was inundated with friends ringing her up that morning to say that they had heard it. It is staggering just how wide an audience the major radio and TV programmes have.

We chose to walk back to the hotel that morning as the weather was pleasant and we had had little opportunity for any exercise at all to date. Warsaw was a very attractive city. We had a good look round the old town, which had been painstakingly renovated to resemble its pre-war state. To be precise, it was rebuilt to resemble the way it looked in the seventeenth and eighteenth centuries, with a positive decision taken not to replace anything that had been built in later years. I must say that the restorers had done an absolutely fabulous job and I can see why it boasts that UNESCO have officially nominated it as one of the world's cultural treasures. As we walked through to the more modern areas of the city, we continued to be impressed with the huge amount of successful renovation and new building work that had already been completed. There were many international firms represented on the streets of Warsaw, which I felt underlined their commitment to Poland's re-emergence.

Because of our early start it was still only 11 a.m. when we got back to the hotel. We were greeted by a representative from RSCG, who had arranged for a mechanic to look at the Healey. This was one of the very rare occasions on the trip where Nawal and I parted company for a while. Nawal went off with the car. It turned out that the mechanic was one of the few people in Poland who really did know about classic cars. He had been a rally driver in the West.

In the meantime I had a good look around the city. Our hotel was located close to the Royal Way – a famous 3-mile route between the Royal Castle and the Royal Summer Palace. I covered a portion of this route which contained many sites of architectural interest. These included fine churches and many monuments to old Polish heroes. Next to our hotel was Pilsudski Square, which contained the

Tomb of the Unknown Soldier. By coincidence I was there in time to see the ceremonial changing of the guard. The tomb is surrounded by very attractive 'English' gardens which I ambled through on my way back to the hotel, soaking up the sunshine and thinking how lucky I was. Already I had seen sights that I was unlikely to see again, met very interesting people, fallen in love with Warsaw – and the best was yet to come. At least it would be, providing we could resolve our problems one step at a time – starting with our oil loss. I returned to the Europejski Hotel expecting Nawal to be there but there was no sign of him. Was this good news or bad? I called home and heard that several more people had telephoned Jenny to comment on the Radio 5 interview. Radio 5 said that they would take up our story again once we had reached Moscow.

I was still a little concerned about the lack of communication we would have with home once we crossed into Siberia. Linked to this concern, I was still worried as to our back-up plan should we have an accident. In fact we hadn't got a back-up plan at all – that was the problem. I had visions of us rolling off the road, with Nawal concussed and me with a broken leg as the car lay upside down in a Siberian forest. I think it must have been the excessive vodka the previous night which caused an overactive imagination on my part. I thought that if we were in trouble then it would be helpful to be able to contact someone. At least they would know where we were and would get someone to find us eventually. I had an idea that I may be able to borrow a satellite phone from the BBC. When we had been organising the trip I had made enquiries as to whether my ordinary GPS car telephone would be effective. I found out that although this would work in certain far-flung places such as Hong Kong, apparently it would not operate in either Russia or China. When I tried to obtain a satellite phone from home I eventually tracked one down but was quoted £4,000 just to borrow it. Maybe the BBC was the answer. If they found our story interesting then surely they would find it helpful if I phoned them from the

45

Russian steppes or some other remote area every so often. I made a mental note to contact Sanchia Berg again to find out the name of the BBC's Moscow correspondent.

While I was thinking through these points Nawal reappeared. The car did not have a broken piston ring – which was a relief, providing we could identify the problem. Apparently we could. One of the oil inlets in the rocker cover was too big and therefore it was letting in an excessive amount of oil. The oil had nowhere to go except to be pumped straight out of the outlet pipe and, eventually, on to the road beneath. Our friendly Polish mechanic had hammered the hole smaller and this might or might not improve matters. In any case, if we kept below about 3,500 revs, the pressure wasn't great enough to cause the overspill. Given the likelihood of ever worsening road conditions ahead, then our speed would undoubtedly be much slower than on the German autobahn. Therefore, the discipline of travelling no more than about 40-45 m.p.h. was not a problem.

That evening, feeling a lot better, we went to the private flat of Edyka Bachs, the boss of the PR team, and had another extremely pleasant evening: good food, good wine, good background music and very interesting conversation. Edyka's partner was an artist and there was something of a Bohemian atmosphere throughout the evening. That was coupled with a lot of detailed talk about the positive prospects for Poland from this crowd of young people representing the very generation on which the future of this fascinating country depends. Although having no connections with Poland myself I nevertheless empathised with them and desperately hoped that Polish optimism, epitomised in the talk that evening, would not be dashed in the years ahead as had been the case so many times in its tumultuous past. We rolled back to the hotel at about 2 a.m.

The next morning after breakfast I tried to contact Cadbury's Belarus agent. Our next stop would be Minsk but we still had no confirmation of our hotel, whether they were going to meet us at the border or whether they would supply us with fuel throughout our passage across Belarus as they had indicated in earlier telephone conversations to the UK.

Although this was just one example, I did find myself having to spend a great deal of time each day simply confirming (or arranging from scratch!) the next day's proceedings. It wasn't just a case of getting in the car when we were ready and setting off. Many arrangements had to be made 'on the hoof', and contact with the right person, or often any person at all, wasn't always easy. In fact, this is what proved to be the case on this occasion. Try as I might, I just couldn't get through on the number given. I called Chris Capstick in Birmingham and was given an alternative number. I eventually managed to get through to Vadym in Minsk, who said that he would fax us details of procedures and would ensure that someone met us at the border. He gave us the name of our hotel in Minsk: the Planeta. I agreed to fax him the details of the press conference that had been arranged for us in Warsaw, to make it easier for him to do the same thing for the benefit of his company. This was precisely what he wanted to do but he really had no clue as to how to organise a press conference. He also said that border crossings, even with the right papers, had been known to take days in some cases! On that reassuring note I put the phone down! I was still hoping to make it from Warsaw to Minsk in one day and wasn't banking on anything more than an hour at the border. Ah well, we'll just have to wait and see, I thought.

At this point, despite the fact we had spent extra time repairing the car, we were actually ahead of schedule. This was mainly because, regrettably, we had had to cancel our detour to southern Poland. A little later that evening I received a fax from Minsk which appeared to ensure that our border crossing would be smooth. It was always difficult to translate the meaning of these fax messages because the literal English translation often did not make sense. In this case, for example, the message had concluded 'all is well and smooth with the frontiers'. That could have meant that the road surface was smooth, because that was another question that we had posed. It could have meant that people, in general, were still getting across, because we knew that sometimes they closed the border. However, whenever there was a choice of interpretation we always chose the most optimistic alternative. We chose to believe, in this case, that Vadym had squared it with the border guards, that Vadym and team would meet us at the frontier and that we should have to spend little time on the crossing itself. At the back of our minds I suspect we knew we were kidding ourselves a bit, but at least it postponed having to sort out any fresh problem at that stage.

We also heard from Moscow that they were organising a press conference for three days after the date on which we were now likely to arrive. We were both keen to spend as little time as possible in Russia because we really wanted to take time to explore China. Neither of us had been to China before. We therefore wanted to try and persuade Moscow to bring the conference date earlier. Yet another matter that required some time to resolve!

However, all these detailed concerns were as nothing to the difficulties that we faced when we read our next incoming fax – this time from China.

When we were at the planning stage in the UK, Cadbury's China had asked us to pay them US$1,500 as the cost of obtaining the Chinese visa. Once again we found that the unique nature of our trip meant that there was no standardised method for obtaining the necessary documentation. We were not flying to Italy, Morocco or the States, following in the footsteps of thousands of travellers before us. In these cases the bureaucratic procedures have been adhered to so many times that there is a well-known and standard procedure. As my earlier phone call to the Chinese embassy in London reminded me, foreigners do not drive to China. A visa for such an event is subject to discussion with all those who have influence on the border guards and other relevant officials. There is no standard procedure.

There is no standard cost. US$1,500 seemed a steep enough price to pay, but a week before we departed we were informed that the total cost was actually $2,000. We took a deep breath and paid up! Our latest fax informed us that they were still fairly confident that they could negotiate successfully to obtain a visa but we would need to pay an additional *$11,000*! There was a complicated story relating to the bankruptcy of the first 'travel agent' but this in itself did not account for the huge additional demand. What was clear was a final comment from Cadbury's stating that in view of this huge increase they were not prepared to put any more money into this project so we had better make alternative arrangements and plan on 'turning around at Moscow'.

This really was a body blow. Perhaps if we had been aware of these problems long before we left England then we could have been in a better position to consider alternative destinations. To be advised, not only after all the preparations had been completed, but actually one week into the trip itself, was a very difficult pill to swallow. What could we possibly do to raise this sort of money and was it worth it anyway? At the back of my mind was the fact that there was still no certainty that even this huge sum would guarantee the necessary entry visa. But, there again, there were never any guarantees on a journey like this.

We couldn't think of an immediate solution but were interrupted in our huddled conference by the arrival of two girls from Euro-RSCG. And very attractive young girls they were, I must add! I assume there was never anything suggestive in their proposals but they did say that they had been sent 'to make sure we were having a good time'. Would we like to go for a walk? This is exactly what we did, and in the warm sunshine of that Thursday afternoon we strolled in the nearby park as far as a lake and a small café. Here we sat and had drinks, half the time talking to and enjoying the company of our hosts (or should I say hostesses?) and spending the other half huddled together discussing possible ways of raising more finance. We went back to the Euro-RSCG office at about 8 p.m. and composed and despatched a series of faxes. We asked the Cadbury's MD for the Pacific region if there was any further give on their part and asked him to telephone us, at any time during the night which suited him, in order to discuss the situation. We also asked most of our minor sponsors and other agents of Cadbury's whether they would be prepared to contribute a little more. Nawal was rather good at persuasion and he spent some considerable time on the phone to a variety of sources. We terminated the evening feeling slightly more hopeful that we might be able to pull something out of the bag but we were still a long way short of sufficient firm commitments. At about 11 p.m. we gave up for the day and went back with all our new-found friends, about a dozen of us all told at this stage, to the Blue Cactus. This was the nightclub where we had spent such an enjoyable evening on our first day in Warsaw. That seemed ages ago but in fact had been only three days earlier. We drank our troubles away and crawled back to the hotel in the small hours again.

In the morning we felt gloomy. Our mood wasn't helped by the fact that we had received no telephone call from Barry Kitchener in Australia. We had, however, received a fax from him which politely but briefly repeated that he could not commit the firm to any further investment in this project.

We had also received a response from China to our request for a breakdown of the cost of this extra demand. It was just as expected, running along the lines of: entertainment for border guards $2,000; cost of discussions with local commandant $1,000; gross profit for the agent $1,000 etc., etc. In other words it was all, effectively, put down to bribes. It did include one amusing line, namely: all road taxes and likely fines along the route $1,500. I guess it's a different world in China! It's interesting to note that after the completion of our trip a rally was organised from Beijing to Paris. This took a different route as it travelled much further south across the old silk route. It was also a very different type of journey to ours, given the number of support vehicles and the mutual help and pre-booked arrangements made for a larger party. I spoke to the organisers and it turns out that they had to pay about £7,500 per car per exit from China, so perhaps there is some consistency in visa costs after all.

As we departed Warsaw for Minsk I began to consider alternative destinations. Perhaps we could reach Moscow then travel due north and up to the Arctic Circle and see the northern lights. There again, perhaps we should head south from Moscow and drive down to Turkey. Both exciting trips but, in my view, both falling well short of our original objective of Beijing. Besides, we both felt we were committed to reaching China. We had told everyone that that was where we were going. We had arranged to wave the flag for Children in Crisis as far as their plans to open an orphanage in China were concerned. Neither of us was at all keen on altering our schedule at this late stage.

We departed Warsaw heading east for the border. Our journey throughout Poland had been consistently due east through the centre of the country and we had therefore missed the more attractive scenery of the mountains in the south and the scenic coastal region to the north. Instead we were treated to the dull and unending vista of Poland's vast central plain.

We took just half an hour to get across the border into Belarus. Was this a record, I wondered, given all that I had heard about the lengthy delays that were the norm? We had heard a rumour that the next border, into Russia itself, was very easy indeed. Despite the break-up of the Soviet Union, Belarus and Russia maintained such close relations that entry into one ensured easy passage into the next. We heard from various native Belarussians during our stay that, despite popular feelings to the contrary, it was quite probable that the country's rulers would agree ever closer ties with Russia. This was in marked contrast to the Polish policy of distancing themselves as rapidly as possible from

51

their eastern neighbours and tying themselves ever closer to the West.

We filled up with petrol for the princely sum of $6. The whole process of topping up with petrol was an education in itself. At this stage of the journey petrol stations were still fairly easily recognisable – not the case a couple of thousand miles further on. The problem was that it wasn't clear which strength of petrol was available on each pump. The second problem was that the filling stations were extremely security conscious. Attendants sat behind thick bulletproof glass with a rickety old metal scoop to push under the tiny aperture to receive our rubles. We needed to state exactly how much petrol we required (we couldn't say, 'Just fill her up'). Nobody spoke English so our requirements had to be expressed in Russian. Rather like the Russian embassy staff in London, there was absolutely no sense of service to the customer. However well we acted and showed our fingers to indicate numbers of litres, they would do absolutely nothing until we gave the full and correct phraseology in their own language. Fortunately, the Berlitz phrase books covered these points and I swiftly learnt, and shall remember to my dying day, the Russian for '30 litres of 93 octane, please'. This was a vital phrase on our trip at the time but hardly likely to form the centrepiece of an animated conversation with any Russians whom I may happen to come across later in the UK!

The final surprise at the filling station was due to the nozzle of the pumps being very wide and the fact that there is no subtle balance in between full on or full off. Conversely the filler pipe of the Healey was significantly smaller than that of the average Russian truck. All this resulted in the fact that on most fills a large portion of our precious fuel was pumped directly over the car, the nearby countryside and us.

We had a further 200 miles to go to Minsk and I was just completing my calculation that we should be there by 6 p.m. when we saw a giant lumber truck heading straight towards us. The road was quite smooth at this point and we were exceeding our suggested maximum speed and were travelling at about 50 m.p.h. We realised that having negotiated a lengthy stretch of road under repair we were now on the wrong side of a dual carriageway. We swiftly cut across the central grass verge and continued on our way. I don't think that this error was quite as stupid as it sounds. Although the roads on this leg of the journey had some good stretches with a smooth(ish) tarmac covering, there was still confusion as to road signs, and even uncertainty if one was travelling through the centre of roadworks. It was difficult to tell. There is absolutely no comparison between the highly organised and standardised road systems and warning signs of Western Europe and the rather ramshackle and underfunded system of the old Soviet countries.

The landscape in Belarus continued to be uninspiring in that the vast flat plains of our last several travelling days continued. However, there were increasing stretches of fir, pine and silver birch forests which succeeded in breaking up the monotony.

We stopped at a roadside café. This was a disused railway truck and was identical to many others that we were to see on our journey right across the country. The only food available was being cooked on a skewer on a small barbecue at the front. We assumed at the time that it was venison. I suspect that at that stage of the journey we were still a little naïve. We later discovered that it was probably dog. Anyway, it was cooked thoroughly so we assumed it must be relatively germ-free. We washed it down with some vodka and some heavy dark-coloured bread. Lunch cost $1 per person and tea was free. Several scruffy children appeared from nowhere and were interested in the car but were very shy. We gave them a handful of sweets. Being sponsored by Cadbury's meant that we had to take a large bag of sweets with us with the expressed intention of distributing them in small batches along the way. Although this took up some of our precious space, it did prove to be a useful conversation opener if we wanted to ask about the route or availability of food etc.

There seemed to be an endless stream of broken-down vehicles, either abandoned or being worked upon, along the side of the road. We made a comfort stop (as the Americans would say) on one occasion next to some trees. There was a man sitting by his broken-down Lada, just staring into space. 'I am a Yugoslav,' he explained. 'My car is broken but I have no money to repair it.' I presume he was telling the truth. I wonder how many other sorry tales existed amongst the numerous little clumps of bedraggled humanity that we passed along the roadside, all trying to make it to a better life in the big cities – in this case Minsk. I didn't know whether to tell him he was better off where he was rather than facing the inevitable disillusionment he would find when in Minsk. I said nothing.

At this stage petrol was available every 30 or 40 miles, so we had no problems in that respect. It generally cost about half the normal UK price.

We arrived in Minsk in the late afternoon and very quickly found the hotel – Hotel Planeta. I had been told by the Belarus consul in London that Minsk was considered to be a city akin in design and ambiance to the great cities of Western Europe. I now realised that he was, to say the least, heavily biased and had used a great deal of poetic licence. Most of Minsk had been destroyed during the war and had been rebuilt in the 1950s and 1960s in typical Soviet style. There were endless massive drab apartment blocks; huge Soviet-style monuments to 'the cause' or 'the struggle' – whatever that was. However, there was a lot of greenery between these various concrete edifices and with the sun brightly shining at the time and the people we met in the streets appearing happy and smiling, then perhaps it wasn't too depressing a place after all. At this stage Nawal and I were being housed in separate hotel rooms, which was a luxury of privacy that we were to lose all too soon as we later entered Asian Russia and hotel costs came within our own personal budget. Our rooms were furnished in a Spartan manner but were clean and functional. Best of all, there was an efficient and modern shower. It was amazing how, after only a week of travel, the simplest of pleasures was considered a real treat. I must have spent half an hour in the shower!

Downstairs we met Vadym and Nino from the distribution company. They were to look after us for our short stay in their country. They greeted us with the good news that they would respond positively to a question we recently put to them in a fax: regarding our Chinese visa problem, they would be prepared to chip in an extra $2,500 in cash. With other small but positive responses from elsewhere we had already cut the $11,000 shortfall to $5,000. Maybe we could close the gap altogether after all.

They told us the plans that they had for us the next day. They were to collect us about 10-ish and take the car to a prominent city centre location where we would be giving out sweets to children. The event would be located outside the local children's theatre and would have media coverage. Further details were discussed and Nawal and I then made our farewells until the morning and went to sample the delights of the hotel restaurant for dinner. The hotel was huge, as was everything else in this city as far as we could see. The restaurant was on the top floor of the hotel and there must have been about 150 tables. It was packed. We waited and were given a table after a few minutes. We were immediately joined by a pretty girl who was keen to talk. It was clear that this form of prostitution was widespread at least in the 'business' hotels. I could hardly call them tourist hotels as we saw very few foreigners in Belarus. There were many girls who looked out of context in relation to their dining companions. Surely the whole of Minsk couldn't be full of rather decrepit old uncles having dinner with their young nieces, could it? We had a rather uninspiring dinner and then I went to bed – alone (honest!).

I woke at 8 a.m. Clocks had moved on another hour, so we were now two hours ahead of England. There was no choice for breakfast but what was presented was good: fried eggs, bread, jam, tea and orange juice. We took everything out of the car and stuffed it into our rooms. This was no easy task in a busy hotel with a small lift. We weren't sure of the safety regulations that should apply when transferring cans of oil and petrol into an hotel bedroom! The most difficult manoeuvring was left for the car's hard top. It was very bulky and was an unusual item to carry through a hotel lobby. We wanted to drive through Minsk city centre with open top thereby allowing as many people as possible to see the car and the promotional material we were to carry within it.

The morning event went smoothly. I realised that the children who had come to watch the show at the theatre were all from various orphanages. There must have been several hundred children. After watching the show ourselves we drove back to the distributor's office and sent more faxes to China, Australia, the charity in London, Birmingham and Moscow. These explained our financial predicament and, in Nawal's subtle phrasing, attempted to squeeze more donations for the cause.

We had been told that Belarus was the poorest of all the European countries – in an even more parlous state than Albania, apparently. That didn't surprise me when observing the various city scenes around us. It wasn't a dirty city compared to some of those found in India or Africa, but it was drab, with little in the way of amenities or products in the shops. We found it all the more surprising, therefore, when we were taken for lunch. Our two young Belarussian executives, looking dapper in their Western suits, drove us out to a nondescript part of the town. We got out of the car in a small car park and entered yet another drab building, but this time single-storey. I noticed that the half-dozen or so cars in the car park were *all* large Mercedes, as was ours. There were a number of burly-looking characters lurking around. We knocked on a door and after some brief discussion were ushered inside. It was just like Aladdin's cave. I was transported back to a scene reminiscent of the best restaurants in the City of London: immaculately dressed waiters and plenty of them, fine linen tablecloths, cut glass and silver cutlery; a range of the world's very best wines

56

and a menu (in French) that would suggest five Egon Ronay stars if it lived up to its promise – which it did. I had beluga caviar with vodka, lobster salad with champagne and a medley of exotic fruits to follow. The coffee and liqueurs were excellent.

This was our first insight into the world of the mafia. I am not at all sure that our hosts were mafiosi in the literal sense of the description but it is true that the lifting of the communist regime had allowed anyone with connections and a bit of business sense to make money. Several had done so and there were a number of multimillionaires living in Belarus, amongst some of the poorest people in Europe. For them money was no object. Our meal must have cost many hundreds of pounds. We found this phenomenon throughout Russia as well, and most of the wealthy class was young.

I suppose that I should have had a conscience sitting in that oasis of luxury with poverty only a few hundred yards away. Herein lies yet another of life's moral dilemmas. Should our hosts be allowed to keep the millions that they obviously had made or should they be taxed heavily as a penalty in order to help their poorer countrymen? Their view was that they paid enough tax as it was. Their ideas and entrepreneurial efforts benefited the state because of the taxes that they paid. They also satisfied a demand from their customers in providing for their needs. To raise taxes further, or to prevent them in other ways from making a profit, would simply push them to operate in another part of the world and the Belarus state, population and they themselves would all be the worse for that. This is, of course, an ideological argument which is debated the world over.

As for my dilemma – how could I enjoy a gourmet meal like this, knowing that it cost a year's income for most of the people I would meet outside? I suppose my answer to that is that proximity to poverty shouldn't make all that much difference. I would have enjoyed the meal in London without giving it a thought. What difference does it make being nearer to poverty, if you know world poverty exists wherever you happen to be? Surely all Westerners should have a conscience as they live a life of relative luxury whilst many in the world starve or die of diseases that cost little to cure. Again, this is one of the big moral questions of our age and there is no easy answer.

After lunch we were taken to a press conference which included both newspaper and TV reporters. We saw ourselves on the hotel TV a few hours later. I really couldn't think of myself either as a pioneer or as a crusading charity worker. Yet this, presumably, is what we were being built up to be with all this media attention. Our next meeting brought us right back to the humble reality of our true status.

Because we were raising some of our money to give towards the Children of Chernobyl charity, some of the charity workers from the local office were present at the conference and later took us to see their work. They explained what had happened ten years ago when the reactor exploded. These people were examples of the true saints of our day and age, working for free, ceaselessly and with very limited resources, in a poor country, against overwhelming odds to try and counteract the damage caused by this accident. Our tiny cash contribution to this cause was totally overshadowed by the efforts that they put in day after day.

On 26 April 1986 the worst nuclear accident in history occurred at the Chernobyl nuclear power plant in the Ukraine, barely 7 miles south of the Belarussian border. The prevailing winds blow northwards. The explosion of the fourth reactor of the plant, initially concealed by the Soviet authorities, spread radioactive pollution across large portions of Belarus. In the first days of the explosion the level of gamma radiation exceeded natural values by 25 times in the capital Minsk and by 1,500 times in the southern town of Bragin. Within two weeks of the disaster radioactive pollution spread as far as Italy in the south, Norway in the north and the British Isles in the west. Yet Belarus was by far the hardest hit. Its effects were uneven. There was resettlement for many but money ran out and this ceased. In general every fifth Belarussian still lives in a contaminated area. Most of them continue to eat domestic farm produce, thus building up radionuclides in their bodies. Officially, the accident resulted in 30 deaths. Only now are the much larger widespread long-term effects being realised. Cases of thyroid cancer in children increased from just two in 1986 to several hundred in 1996. This is just one example of the known (and it is suspected that there are many unknown) long-term genetic effects of this tragedy. Belarus is desperately short of the medical equipment needed to monitor and counteract these problems. It is estimated that these genetic problems will still be evident even three or four generations from now.

The problems that this caused to the weaker and less resistant members of society – the sick, the young and the old – was compounded by the fact that pollution was rife before the accident. Lack of any noxious gas emission controls during the Soviet era, in their drive for industrial strength, had resulted in very poor air quality in any event. One of the objects of the charity was to take children away from their environment for a minimum of a month at a time. When we were there a couple from Ireland were visiting as they had been short-term foster parents to local children for several years and were coming to collect another batch of six children for a month's holiday at their farm in county Kerry. They were also there to discuss the logistics of leasing a plane later that summer to fly 60 to 70 children to various homes scattered around south-western Ireland.

Scientists estimated that a month in a clean environment such as that that existed in most parts of the British Isles would add between two and four years to the life of a young child. Again we were humbled. The simple right for us in England to breathe relatively clean air is taken for granted. This is a basic requirement for a healthy life and yet many children were denied even that. Travel broadens the mind and this was just one of several rather sober moments for me as I realised what a charmed life I had really been allowed to live compared to so many other people in the world.

We returned to the hotel once our discussions with the charity workers had finished. We were due to meet them again the next day. On the way to the hotel I wanted to buy some postage stamps in order to send about a dozen postcards to England. Even this seemingly simple procedure was fraught with difficulty. Fortunately we had Vadym in the vehicle, who knew his way around Minsk and, of course, could speak the language. It nevertheless took us some time to find a post office that actually had stamps for sale and when we did they were unable to supply the correct value. It was complicated enough even with Vadym there to sort it out for us; it would have been almost impossible should we have been on our own.

Nawal and I tried to find a reasonable restaurant that evening for dinner but, apart from a very few extremely expensive ones, our only hope was back at the hotel again. It seemed that the average citizen of Minsk just did not eat out. Presumably it was too expensive.

I found it difficult to sleep that night; perhaps it was the length of daylight hours. It got light at about 4 a.m. Over breakfast we reviewed how the trip had gone so far. It was frustrating to know that with the vast bulk of the miles still ahead of us we had only been travelling for three out of the eight days since we left home. However, we recognised that with three of our major sponsors located within a couple of days' drive of each other, then we would have to be patient until we left Moscow. Then we could travel as fast as we liked, subject only to road conditions. I had found that my normal go-go temperament was being forced into a different pace. I had to learn to relax. When we were with local agents, who were, after all, paying for a large part of that segment of the trip, then the decision to move on was, to a large extent, taken out of our hands. I was also becoming more philosophical when considering our various mechanical and other problems. Our major problem of the extra cost for the Chinese visa was looking more hopeful. We put in a little more money ourselves and hoped we could talk Moscow into contributing the remaining balance. We thought that we would have a creditable argument in that we had already found $8,000 of the required $11,000 dollars whilst on our trip. No mean feat really. On that basis, another couple of thousand from them would not seem too bad. How could they refuse, we thought.

I found that I was enjoying the trip more and more. It was an adventure and the few problems that we had had were already largely resolved. It was quite a satisfying feeling. We were now meeting people who knew a little bit about the next leg of our journey. This was a common theme throughout our trip. It meant that we were reasonably sure about the next day's drive but that we could never really plan too far ahead with any confidence. I found that we were still getting contradictory reports. For example, we met an Indian consular official in the hotel car park who had just toured Europe with his family. He said that apart from the odd stretch the roads were fine all the way to Irkutsk. (We still hadn't heard from anybody what it was like the other side of Irkutsk. I was beginning to wonder if the world ended there!) He said that conditions were better than in Poland and that fuel was available all the way across. On security, however, we would need to be careful.

But we also met a US air force colonel, Bob Boswell, who had spent much of his career in Eastern Europe and, more latterly, in Belarus and Russia. He was very much more uncertain that we would find the roads adequate or that fuel could be relied upon.

That afternoon we again met Valentina, who ran the Chernobyl charity. She took us to a little chapel of remembrance that had been established as an interdenominational house of God where anyone could come and pray for the victims of the disaster. This was situated in a local park which had itself been dedicated to this cause. It was very moving.

Much later that afternoon Vadym and his wife called for

61

us and the four of us went in the now open-topped Healey for a drive round the main sights of the city. We were stopped by the police for driving down the wrong side of the road and we didn't have our driving licences with us, which is, apparently, almost a hanging offence. However, after some stressing of the charitable nature of our project, the policeman waved us on.

That evening Nawal detailed me to get a position fix, using the GPS system, on our next few objectives. I didn't believe that this would be helpful at all. What is the use of knowing the map co-ordinates for Moscow, for example? What we wanted was to speak to Vadym to ask for directions to take us to the Moscow road. Having been with Nawal for ten days now, this was one of those times when I was beginning to find him infuriating. He insisted on having his own way and it didn't help that he was never complimentary to others when they came up with an improved solution. However, his background was very different to mine and I suppose different people act in different ways. I went off to find a bit of clear sky in the park in order to get the position fixes – not because they would be of any use, but because it was a good excuse to get an hour's break from Nawal. I have to repeat, though, that the times like this when I felt claustrophobic were relatively few. I remained pleasantly surprised, in fact, by the length of time we spent together in perfect harmony and, often, in laughter. When I considered that I had never spent so much time continuously with anyone I was, overall, pleased with our relationship.

The next day was Monday, 3 June – Jenny's birthday. I woke up thinking about her and how much I missed her and the family. She had been particularly supportive when organising this trip and I knew that she really wanted me to get the most out of this rare opportunity. It was as much for her as for me that I really wanted to make a success of the trip. If we got to Moscow, which now seemed almost a certainty, then that would at least have achieved the minimum that I had hoped for from the trip. But the real prize lay much further ahead. I couldn't wait to cross Russia's eastern border into China. This would be the moment I had been dreaming about and working hard to achieve for some time. Even though we hoped to travel a further 1,500 miles onwards thereafter to the city of Beijing, the crossing of the Sino-Soviet border would be the crowning glory for me.

I got out of bed and clambered over spare tyres, oil cans, rugs and other debris in order to get to the shower. Afterwards I sat down and listed those jobs that we still had to conclude. We still needed to resolve the problem of more funds for the Chinese visa. We also needed to persuade the Chinese ambassador in Moscow to come to the press conference to be held there. We could then, perhaps, get him to smooth our passage over the all-important Sino-Soviet border. I also needed time with Intourist when we got to Moscow in order to get the latest information for our onward route and to try and organise some hotel accommodation in advance. I had a friend working 200 miles to the south-east of the city; I could contact him and, maybe, even spend a night with him. The Belarus agents had two connected companies in Russia, one located in Samara and one in Irkutsk. It would be useful to contact them from Moscow to see if they could help us when travelling through their region. We also wanted to keep everyone in touch with events at home, not only our respective families but also a whole range of other people, including the local press, who seemed to be serialising our story. I therefore composed a number of faxes to be sent from Rostel's offices that morning. Rostel was yet another trading name for the import/export agency within Vadym and Nino's empire.

I pestered Nawal to get a move on as I wanted to make it to their office before 10 a.m. in order to call Jenny and wish her a happy birthday before she left for work (as a teacher) at 8.30 a.m. UK time. This irritated him immensely. 'You already called her yesterday,' he said. That was true but I felt a two-minute call would be just the right touch on her actual birthday morning. Obviously Nawal did not share that view. I had also informed Nawal that the distance to

Smolensk, our interim stop before Moscow, was 120 miles, thinking that it was 200 kilometres away. I later realised that it was 200 miles away not 200 kilometres. When I then explained this to Nawal he exploded. I am not quite sure why because it's not as if I'd pushed Smolensk a little further on just to spite him. If it was 200 miles then it was 200 miles and that was all there was to it. I guessed he was feeling like I did a couple of nights earlier.

In the event, when we got to the office, we found that all international calls to UK, China and even Moscow were impossible to make that morning. We gave up and said our goodbyes. We left Minsk about midday and drove to the Russian border. Apart from being stopped three times for speeding, but luckily only cautioned each time, we made it to the frontier with no further ado. Formalities were minimal but we were asked for a $20 exit fee from the Belarus side. Our explanation of charity work status managed to be sufficient reason for this to be waived.

Shortly after crossing the border we stopped for petrol, which, as in Poland, was much cheaper than in England. We noticed a small petrol tanker parked as though it was in someone's backyard. Sure enough, this was the petrol station. The attendant went to unscrew the nozzle but we stopped him just in time because the cardboard sign above read '76 octane'. We needed 93 or 95 octane, we said. 'No problem', he said, and turned the cardboard sign around so that we could read the other side, which said '93 octane'. He then proceeded to pour it from exactly the same single nozzle outlet! We were so taken aback that it was too late to protest. However, he assured us that it really was 93 octane and I have to admit that we had no problems once on the road again.

The scenery was becoming increasingly more interesting after the empty plains of central Europe. We were now travelling through, if not exactly mountainous areas, at least undulating countryside which created a variety of views. The feeling of emptiness as we gazed ahead to the distant horizon was beginning to be broken up by numbers of wooded areas. We were seeing the start of the forested lands that would become such a feature for us over the next few weeks. We got to Smolensk bang on schedule at 7 p.m. The motel was in its own grounds about half a mile from the city itself and was a very seedy place. It clearly was a truckers' dive, with more prostitutes than drivers. The accommodation was minimal but even the smallest room appears spacious to anyone who has just spent eight hours in an Austin Healey. After a poor meal in the motel's cavernous and rather depressing dining room we went to our bedroom, bolted the door behind us and went straight to sleep.

The next morning we chatted to some of the truck drivers. They represented many nationalities between them. The route from Europe to Moscow was heavily used. A couple of Belgian drivers warned us to be very careful if we were travelling on from Moscow. As far as security at night was concerned, we should be OK if staying in hotels. If we were unable to make it to a hotel then we should drive until we found a couple of truckies settling down for the night and attach ourselves to their 'convoy'. There was safety in numbers.

Our drive to Moscow took a long time. The road was not as good as we had been led to believe and we were stopped twice for minor infringements of the traffic laws. Luckily we managed to talk our way out of it. We had drawn up a sheet of information about our trip and also about the car. We had been asked many a time about the history of the car, its top speed, the engine size etc. To have all this already printed in Russian was extremely useful. We found our-selves handing out these sheets frequently, particularly at the regular police checkpoints.

It was hot as we reached Moscow even though this was to be the most northerly point of our trip. The earlier comments identifying excessive heat as the most likely climatic scenario as we would be crossing the world's largest landmass were already beginning to prove accurate. As we neared the Moscow ring road the traffic began to build up considerably. I knew a little bit about the geography of the city, having visited it on business a few times before. As we reached the central city areas I recognised the Kremlin and felt that we should be travelling in the opposite direction. We stopped to confirm this point and a passing motorist said, in English, 'Follow me.' He took us right to the door of our hotel – The Gorbachov.

I think it was around this time that I was at the peak (or nadir?) of my concern for our safety. Our check-in story was the final straw. As we approached the hotel I noticed that all the shops on this rather smart boulevard had armed guards posted outside. As we got to the hotel we were signalled to stop and the hotel guard, equipped with a gun, gave us a cursory search then waved us on. The great iron gate, rather like a portcullis, swung sideways on its electronic arm. We stopped ahead of the second gate whilst the first closed behind us. Then we were ushered through into the courtyard. When we got out of the car we walked through thick glass doors into the lobby, where yet another armed guard sat in front of the counter. A girl who sat behind the bulletproof glass screen said, 'Welcome to Moscow.' I asked how things were in Moscow. She said they were fine and then asked us how long we were staying. I replied that we would be staying two or maybe three days. I added that we were then travelling further east by car. 'But what about the bandits?' she said. 'Oh, you English, you are so brave.'

That was enough for me. I rushed up to my room. How could a girl who spends her life sitting behind armed guards and bulletproof glass think that I am the one who is brave because I'm travelling east of Moscow? I must have miscalculated. Maybe we shouldn't go further after all, I thought. I immediately phoned home to speak to Jenny and the conversation went something like this:

'Hello darling, it's me. We are in Moscow now and we think we have raised the extra money so we'll probably carry on eastwards from here,' I said in my best and somewhat emotional WW2 going-over-the-top voice.

'Oh good, you'll have a great time,' she said, in a matter-of-fact sort of way.

'Yes, but I think it might be a bit tough. You know I've always loved you, don't you, darling?' I continued.

'Hello, hello. Are you still there, David? I think it's a bad line.'

'And tell the children that I love them all too, won't you?'

'Have you been at the vodka again, David?' she asked.

'Well, darling, I think I better go now . . . bye,' and I put the phone down thinking, 'that's probably the last time I'll ever hear her voice.'

She put the phone down thinking, 'What a jerk, I just hope he sobers up by morning!'

In the afternoon I put a brave face on my thoughts. Nawal didn't seem to have batted an eyelid. We went to visit the Cadbury office and had a long conversation with Peter Kirby, the manager. He was a young fellow and, frankly, no match for Nawal. The conversation began with Peter saying that he had heard about our financial problems but he didn't see what a problem in China had to do with him and he certainly wasn't prepared to put more money into our project. It ended with him giving us $2,500 and agreeing to pay all the Moscow hotel bills! In return we had agreed to do two extra press conferences, one in Novgorod and one in Ekaterinburg. We then made several long-distance phone calls (at his expense!) and returned to the hotel.

That evening we were free and spent the time doing the usual touristy things in Moscow, including taking the metro to Red Square and trying, but failing, to get tickets for the Bolshoi ballet. It was at this stage that I began to reflect on what we had achieved so far. Of course, I am not talking about anything comparable to the true explorers of the world. I realise that we were in a completely different league from all those people who have fought against the elements and been the first to reach a particular point on the globe. I recognise my humble position in terms of exploration. On the other hand, from a purely personal point of view, I felt pleased that I, a middle-aged and pretty average sort of person, had actually driven to Moscow. It was something unusual, particularly as we had done it without any support vehicle and in a 35-year-old car. I wouldn't like to boast about it to someone like Ranulph Fiennes, who crosses the North Pole on foot as a matter of course, but at least it was good enough for half an hour's storytelling in the local pub!

In the morning I thought about the coming day's schedule. This could well be our last day in Moscow. I needed to think through what we had to do in what was beginning to feel like our last stop in civilisation for some considerable time. My mind also wandered further ahead into the unknown of Siberia. I reflected again on the comments from the hotel receptionist – 'but aren't you afraid of the bandits?' I guessed that there wasn't much more that we could have done by that stage. I just hoped that we could be sensible. We didn't want to travel in the dark and we did want to try and get to an hotel each night. I wondered if this is what the old cowboys used to feel in the Wild West of America as they kept their fingers crossed that they wouldn't run into a tribe of Indians during the day and would manage to make it to the next fort by the evening!

Nawal and I met to discuss our next steps. We needed to speak to Ma Dan, the right-hand assistant of Jeff Briggs, the manager of Cadbury's China. She seemed to know what was going on and we needed to know how the 'negotiations' for the visa were faring. We understood that we were to have a press conference when (and if) we reached Beijing to be held right next to the Great Wall of China. We had some thoughts as to how that might be organised, given our new-found expertise on the subject of press conferences. We also wanted to know if it would make a big difference to costs if I were to fly the last leg across the border and join up with Nawal again in China. I needed to speak to Intourist and we also needed to know the detail of what was expected from us in Moscow from Julie Wayne, the PR leader whom Cadbury's had appointed for masterminding our stay in Moscow.

We had a very frustrating morning. It took a great deal of time to plan a new schedule for our onward trip through Russia; a full four hours before I was even halfway satisfied. I then wanted to leave for the Intourist office in order to get information about, and hopefully book, hotel rooms. Cadbury's said that American Express were better so I was taken on a long detour to their office, only to be told that they don't handle hotel accommodation, which can only be booked through Intourist. I was then taken to the wrong Intourist office. It took ages to get to the correct one, which was not worth it as they were unable to help tourists already in Russia! With time running out I gave up and went back to the Cadbury office. At least there was good news there in that Barry Kitchener in Australia had agreed to make up the final shortfall of our Chinese visa cost requirement.

With just one hour to go before we were due to leave the Moscow office, I was introduced to one of the PR clerks, called Victoria. She was a very friendly Russian girl who said that she was responsible for Cadbury's business to the immediate east. Having overheard our plans she realised that, ideally, we needed some contacts east of Moscow. She said that she was sure she could help. She then gave me the names and contact numbers of people in the next four cities in which we had planned to spend the night. She made arrangements with the first one and shortly confirmed that we had been booked for the next evening into a particular hotel (the Rusia) in Nizhniy Novgorod, about 300 miles to the east of Moscow. She also insisted that we call her by phone each evening so that she could hear from us as to our estimated arrival time at the next stop. She would then be able to organise our next night's accommodation for us. This was all excellent news if it worked. In fact it did work very well indeed. For the next two weeks we were able to keep some sort of communication going and were regularly received by someone by name each time we entered the next city. The system began to break down a little once we had passed Irkutsk. (Irkutsk again – I was really beginning to think that there was a huge black hole the other side of that particular city as nobody seemed to know anything about what went on thereafter). Victoria's help for the next 3,000 miles made a huge difference to us.

We left the office for our final commitment. This was a visit to a summer school in the middle of attractive gardens in Moscow. The press were there as usual and this was planned as a question-and-answer session with a panel of children. It was good fun. We had to listen to an ingratiating speech wherein we were thanked for our 'very noble deeds'. I cringed! We distributed sweets to the assembled crowd of enthusiastic schoolchildren and returned to the hotel. We were taken out that evening to the American Bar by Julie and Victoria from the PR company. Why were we lucky enough to have girls as escorts all the time? I wasn't complaining.

Julie, who was the boss of the PR company, said that she had come out to Moscow in 1994 for two months' work experience. She had enjoyed it so much and considered that, with the fall of the Soviet system, there were so many opportunities here, that she stayed on. She was very happy with her new life in Moscow. It must be remembered that the smothering Soviet system, which had prevented any form of economic initiatives and stifled anyone with entre-preneurial aspirations, had only recently collapsed. Few people who were still alive could remember any other system. All of a sudden the lid was off! The younger generation were wildly optimistic about their personal pros-pects and the future of the new 'free' Russia as a whole. No doubt too optimistic, as I suspect the next few years might show, as it is difficult to move a whole country instantly from rags to riches; particularly such a vast country as this, which has inherited very inefficient economic and political structures from the former Soviet days. Some people, per-haps many people, will become disillusioned. But at that time optimism abounded and it was good to see. Victoria, who was a native Russian and had been so helpful to us with onward connections, was just fascinated with what we were attempting to do. She hadn't heard of anyone driving all the way across Siberia. We had a very pleasant evening in this restaurant, which was so typical of the many essentially American-style eating places that had recently burst on to the scene. We returned to the hotel for what would be our final night in Moscow.

The experiences of the trip so far were different to my expectations in that we had spent so much time discussing and debating the business aspects of the project. We had spent a long time composing and sending faxes to England, Warsaw, Minsk, China and Australia. We had been involved in prolonged negotiations in trying to raise an extra $11,000. A lot of time had been spent on the press conferences and promoting the business of our sponsors. An appreciable amount of time had also been spent on very good living – pleasant hotels and excellent restaurants. We had been treated throughout as celebrities. It was true that we had covered 2,000 miles of road already and had had our share of problems such as exhaust pipe damage and oil loss, but this only accounted for perhaps a quarter of the time spent on the trip so far. But when we left Moscow all this was to change!

In the morning we made an early start. We headed north from the hotel, aiming for the Moscow ring road and then the M7. Russian motorways could not be compared with those in the West such as the infamous M25. The eastbound carriageways of the M7 carried very little traffic and the surface was covered in potholes and loose stones. Mind you, the result was somewhat similar – the average speed on the M7 and the English M25, for different reasons, was about 25 m.p.h. We went against the general flow of the traffic as we turned right, not left, away from the main crowd heading back towards Smolensk, Belarus, Poland and beyond towards civilised Europe. 'East of Moscow' was a phrase that we had heard often, usually accompanied by stories of danger and uncertainty. Well, here we were.

This was the real thing. I gave one last thought to my comfortable home and my family then mentally composed myself for the challenges ahead as we headed east into the unknown.

5

Siberia

The number of potholes and loose stones actually lessened as we travelled on. The problem with this was that we were lulled into a false sense of security and built up a bit of speed between potholes. We then dodged the next two or three, only to be jarred into submission as we sailed straight into the fourth one. We found that we could not afford to lose concentration for a moment, which was difficult when faced with miles of empty road and dull scenery.

We stopped at a roadside café (another abandoned railway truck) for tea and what we assumed was salami. I felt much better as a result and realised that I hadn't eaten anything so far that day.

We saw a number of motorists on the way and most were very friendly, often giving us the thumbs-up sign (at least we assumed it was a single thumb and not two fingers!). Many indicated for us to slow down and then gave us cassette tapes of the most awful Russian music as presents. It was a very nice gesture though. We began to reciprocate by giving them English tapes but we saw our limited stocks diminishing rapidly. We then changed tack and resorted to handing back the Russian tape that we had been given by the previous donor. That way we had a constant circulation of tapes, avoided losing our own, kept everyone happy and, best of all, avoided having to listen to those awful Russian ones!

We really hadn't been sure what sort of reaction we would receive from locals. Had they been brought up on a communist diet of anti-imperialism, I had wondered. Were we considered the enemy as they relived the cold war? All my fears proved unfounded, as everyone we met was keen to speak to us and to welcome us to their country. They made it clear that we were certainly a rarity in their part of the world.

We arrived at Nizhniy on time. Actually we arrived one hour earlier than scheduled because, based on information on our maps, I had assumed that we were due to pass through another time zone and we didn't. I phoned our contact from the telephone in the nearest shop. The use of the phone was willingly given to us – and for free. These weren't quite the dour unfriendly Russian peasants that I had conjured up in my imagination back in England! We cashed some dollars at the nearest bank. The banks all seemed very scruffy but inside they were equipped with the latest technology in counterfeit detection. I was told that there were more US dollars circulating in Russia than there were in America. I am sure that this is an exaggeration but it is true that, certainly in this part of Russia, most people appeared to effect their larger transactions at least, in US dollars. I had a nagging feeling that I had miscalculated and that we were missing a bundle or two of dollar bills. It was difficult to make a thorough search of the car and we had forgotten where we had hurriedly stuffed them when packing the car at home.

As usual, many people came over to the car and struck up conversation. They all seemed keen to practise their English. Our local contact appeared and made himself known to us. He then drove ahead of us to our hotel, where he had made prior arrangements for our stay. Overnight accommodation in Russia is expensive, particularly when considering the very basic and often dirty facilities. This middle of the range hotel in a relatively unimportant city charged $80 per night but we had managed to get a discount as a result of our contact's connections and were charged $55. Already Victoria's help was beginning to pay off for us. This was the first of many occasions when we felt especially grateful for her last-minute intervention.

Cadbury's had an agent in Nizhniy, who called for us at

about 5 p.m. and we were whisked to a press conference, which finished just an hour later. Again we happened to see ourselves on TV as we returned to the hotel. It seems that all regions in Russia enjoy not only their own newspapers but also, usually, their own local TV stations. Nizhniy was a very pleasant city – at least judging from the limited time we had for sightseeing. In this case it was little more than keeping our eyes open as we drove to and from our hotel. I was surprised to read in our Lonely Planet guide that Nizhniy is Russia's third largest city and one of its oldest, being founded in 1221. It was called Gorky in the Soviet era, after the writer Maxim Gorky. Its more recent claim to fame is that it is the city to which the 'dissident' physicist Andrey Sakharov was exiled in 1986. It was, indeed, a big and bustling city and our hotel had a wonderful view directly overlooking the Volga river. We went to bed tired and still waiting to hear from Victoria about our next rendezvous in Ufa. We had an early start in the morning, aiming to get away by 4 a.m., because Ufa was 500 miles away and nobody in Nizhniy was at all sure of the road conditions.

It was already clear that we had entered a completely different phase of our trip. This was the endurance test. Gone were the pamperings of the 'noble charity workers'. From here on it was just one long slog to reach the Chinese border. My schedule, drawn up hurriedly in the Moscow office, called for us to cover long distances on all but two of the next fourteen days.

We started to settle into something of a routine. Each of us by now knew instinctively what the other expected of him. Although I took an occasional turn at the wheel, Nawal preferred to drive and I didn't mind either way. I always had a lot to do. One minute I was checking the road surface ahead and the next checking the rear view which was impossible through the rear window due to the baggage. I was constantly shuffling around in cramped conditions to find the compass or the next map or the thermos flask or a sweet. I would tend to do the 'negotiating' at a petrol stop and, if necessary, ask directions.

We learnt the odd Russian phrase. The word that sticks in my mind is *priama*, which means 'straight on'. Whenever we asked for directions the reply would be to point to the horizon and say, *'Priama, priama.'* This meant you just go on and on. We did!

On Friday we woke at 3.30 a.m. but by the time we had had a cup of tea and thoroughly checked the car it was 5 a.m. We left Nizhniy and made good time. Despite the desire to keep the speed down a bit to reduce the oil spillage, we were tempted to travel at 60 m.p.h. for long stretches as, for a change, the road surface allowed us to do so. After 210 miles with the tank now flickering on empty (fuel gauges rarely work accurately on Healeys!) we turned a corner just before entering the town of Kazan to find ourselves at the back of a stationary queue of traffic. Apparently we had to take a ferry across a very wide river. This was not marked on the map. We waited for over an hour before driving on to the ferry for the short crossing. All other vehicles were high-wheel based as was just about every vehicle that we saw thereafter. I could see why this was the preferred configuration. When we drove off the ferry at the other side a heavy lorry was just ahead of us. As soon as it had cleared the down ramp the whole ferry shifted upwards with this release of weight, catching our exhaust pipe and rupturing it just ahead of the silencer. We disembarked and then stopped. It started to rain, at which point Nawal discovered that he had left his waterproof jacket back in Moscow. We'd had a good start to the day but with precious time wasted and a repair job still to complete we were getting a bit frustrated. We found an empty tin can in the roadside ditch and after a rather skilful piece of surgery managed to clamp it round the gaping hole and sealed it up with a bit of gum. Although not perfect, that seemed to do the trick.

The clocks did have to move forward that day, which shortened the time available to us. At 2 p.m. with 350 miles and difficult road conditions still to come, we set off again. We skirted the old Tatar city of Kazan on our way to Ufa and again started to make good progress. We were both very hungry and there was no sign of habitation, let alone a café. At that point we found that the condition of the road surface deteriorated significantly. We started on what turned out to be 50 miles of road under repair. An ominous rattle developed under the car, which got progressively noisier as we continued. At one point, a particularly loud crunch made us both think that we had broken a suspension leaf. It began to get dark but we couldn't travel any faster. We got to the hotel at what we thought was 11.30 at night but in fact it was half past midnight as we had somehow managed to travel through two time zones that day. It was amazing that nobody in Nizhniy could answer our simple question as to what was the time in the neighbouring city of Ufa.

It took ages to check in despite the lateness of the hour and we were charged $120 for the night. The $4 that Nawal gave a guard to keep an eye on the car overnight seemed better value. We were starving but all restaurants had closed long ago. We were invited to the private quarters of the floor manageress. She was a very pleasant and well-educated lady. She gave us a meal of vegetables, salad, meat and bread. She was perfectly charming and quietly explained how difficult life was for the average Russian. She didn't really have to tell us that as it was obvious from all we had seen so far. She was very unsure about her own future as well as the future of the country. Russia's initial flirtation with a free market economy had been of no benefit to the average Russian. In fact many had seen their life savings drastically reduced in value. She herself had gained a medical degree at a local university some years ago. However, there were simply no jobs available in the medical profession and she had had to make do with working for this hotel. She had a son at school and her sole concern was to give him a good education. Was there any way we could arrange for him to come to Britain to be educated there?

Yet again, I started to think how it is almost a national pastime for us British to be critical of our own country. Yet here we seem to be the envy of the world. Once again, the many little freedoms and luxuries that we often take for granted are not easily come by in other parts of the world. We had a fascinating discussion. An exchange of ideas and a swapping of life stories was perhaps a more accurate description. How different life is for these people, I thought, as we eventually went to bed, absolutely exhausted, at about 3.30 a.m.

We still had to be up by 8.30 a.m. and I awoke worrying about our missing dollars. I was sure we had lost a bundle or two somewhere. The matter was of concern to me because our expenditure on overnight accommodation had been budgeted at $50 per night and we were frequently having to spend considerably more than that. Nobody seemed to be prepared to cash traveller's cheques or to accept credit cards, which were our two standbys in case of emergency. In addition, I was considering that we might have to spend more than budgeted on car repairs, given the frequency, so far, of mechanical problems. We didn't want to add to our concerns about the car by running out of money.

I made the great mistake of telling Nawal about my money worries. I said that I thought we must have lost a couple of bundles as I couldn't get the figures to reconcile. 'That's your responsibility,' he snapped back and wasn't interested in having anything more to do with the problem. I shrugged. I surprised myself by not getting cross with this childish and unhelpful reaction. I was pleased that I was becoming more philosophical. In fact, despite the constant tension that a trip like this creates, I was actually relaxing in myself more and more.

Nawal decided to go to a mechanic (the brother of our friendly floor manageress) to recheck our patch on the exhaust. If we were to make our next stop at Chelyabinsk by that night then I calculated that we would have to leave Ufa by noon. At 1 p.m. there was still no sign of Nawal. Ah well, I thought, another late night. I sat in the park opposite the hotel and soaked up the sunshine. Apart from a brief walk way back in Warsaw, this was the first time I had had any free time to myself. It was a great feeling so part of me didn't want Nawal to return for some time yet.

I wandered into the hotel to see if anyone knew what we might expect on our journey to Chelyabinsk. Predictably, neither the hotel staff nor the sundry guests milling about the foyer knew anything. That really was quite strange when you consider that it was their neighbouring city. The manager thought that it was south of Ufa but the cashier thought it was to the east! Even I could tell from my map that it was due east and it was only 250 miles away. But with that uncertainty amongst the locals what hope had I got of obtaining an honest response to my questions about road conditions or even time zones? Somebody said they thought it would take us four hours, whilst someone else said about ten. As to the time, some people agreed that it was probably on Moscow time. The fact that we were already two hours ahead of Moscow and Chelyabinsk was even further east meant that this clearly didn't make sense. The only explanation I can give is that people just never travelled outside their local community. There was, perhaps, no reason to do so and anyway, in Soviet times, travel was frowned upon, often forbidden, with internal frontier posts established right across the country. In fact some cities, usually those that produced armaments, had been totally off limits to non-resident Russians, let alone foreigners.

Nawal eventually returned just after 3 p.m. by which time I had checked out of the hotel, exchanged some US dollars for rubles, organised a sandwich lunch and packed up.

We left at 4 p.m. but, for a change, we encountered no problems on the roads and made the 250-mile journey in six hours. We had already left Europe behind and were now in Asia. Shortly after that, when crossing the Ural Mountains on this leg of our journey, we officially entered Siberia. The phrase 'the Ural Mountains' was something I first heard at school in my geography lessons and even in my youth they created an aura of mystique in my mind's eye. I had always thought that they marked the edge of the civilised world as we knew it, and here we were about to cross them! I hate to disappoint the reader but in the event, although the crossing of the Urals was a significant moment in our odyssey, the mountains themselves were a bit of a disappointment. Few of them, apparently, are over 3,000 feet in height and most are little more than rolling hills.

Siberia has been described by Maxim Gorky as 'the land of chains and ice', which is, indeed, the typical impression that most people have of this vast land. But it is certainly not accurate – at least in the summertime in this southern part of the region. Siberia really is a huge territory covering more acres than the whole of Europe and the USA combined (5.5 million square miles, for those who like precise numbers!). It contains 53,000 rivers and over 1 million lakes. One of the lakes – the beautiful and serene Lake Baikal – contains 20 per cent of all the world's fresh water. The sheer scale of the region is simply immense. We travelled over 3,000 miles through Siberia, much of the journey being through the taiga – an area of dense forests containing many birch, pine, fir, spruce and larch trees. But there are also lengthy stretches of open scenery – the famous Russian steppes. These flat undulating grasslands stretch south to Russia's border with Outer Mongolia and beyond. The Russian word for Siberia – Sibir – translates as the 'sleeping land'. Siberia contains some sizeable cities, but my abiding memory is one of vast distances with not a soul to be seen. In my mind's eye I can vividly recall the feeling of the overpowering dominance of nature with our tiny car inching its way towards the horizon like an ant crawling across a gigantic carpet.

Svetlana and husband, the two local agents for United Campaigns, the Moscow-based PR company, met us at the police checkpoint on the outskirts of Chelyabinsk. They escorted us to our hotel. It was pleasant but very basic. But then again it cost only $18 as against the previous night's cost of $120 for just three hours' sleep. I was getting used to little food (which was undoubtedly doing me good) and little sleep (which was not). I washed my clothes and was in bed by 1.30 a.m.

One of the problems I had to live with as návigator was that the names of the cities often had different spellings. The city that we had just entered, for example, was named Chelya Binsk on one map and C'elabinsk on another. I often found that a range of names applied to the same city and some of these names bore no resemblance to the others. It was guesswork as to which was the familiar local name when asking the locals for directions. Of course, this was just for phonetic purposes. It was impossible to write anything down because the Russian Cyrillic alphabet contains many different symbols compared to our own. I had been used to finding my way round cities in Europe even though I didn't always speak the language because the written word can be recognised and therefore the signposts are comprehensible. In Russia (and also later on in China) the written word was little better for us than a child's scribble. I had ensured that I had the Russian lettering for each of the cities where we would be staying but the intervening towns were unknown to me in Cyrillic and the final destinations were often spelt differently by the locals. All this added a little bit of extra interest to the life of the Trans-Siberian navigator!

Cadbury's Moscow were the weak link in our chain. It's true they came up trumps with some extra cash and did, after some persuasion, pay our Moscow hotel bills. But they had been very slow in getting our Russian invitation faxed to England, which cost us money and time; they did nothing about our hotels across Russia; and neither of their recommendations – American Express and Intourist – had been able to help us in this respect. We were very fortunate that Victoria Ushakova from United Campaigns came to our rescue at the last minute. Certainly the arrangements had been fine so far. The chain had not broken.

In the morning Svetlana and her husband called as promised and gave us a swift sightseeing tour of their city –

Chelyabinsk. They were very kind to take time out in order to do so. It was always interesting to see how other people lived and to see with our own eyes the local facilities and attractions. Having said that, I would strongly advise against anyone aiming to make Chelyabinsk the centre of their next summer holiday. There really was little of interest and I would hate to have to live there. Chelyabinsk used to be the end of the line (in more ways than one!) as it marked the terminus of the railway from Moscow. However, almost a hundred years earlier Tsar Alexander III authorised the extension of this route further east, which swiftly expanded all the way to Vladivostok on the Pacific coast and this became known as the famous Trans-Siberian Railway. Even to this day the railway is the major method for the transportation of goods across Siberia; people travel by plane.

We left Chelyabinsk at noon en route for Tyumen. We had originally hoped to travel through Ekaterinburg because this city seemed to have enjoyed more than its fair share of history and was, anyway, reputed to be an attractive place. It was originally called Sverdlovsk. This is where Tsar Nicholas II his family were murdered in 1918 and, a little more recently, was the area where Gary Powers of U2 spy plane fame was shot down in 1960. It was also the birthplace of President Yeltsin. Few Russians, let alone foreigners, had visited Ekaterinburg, as it was a closed city until as recently as 1990 because of its armament factories. However, we judged that time was too short to effect this detour and we struggled on towards Tyumen.

En route the screw for my door handle decided to shear off for no particular reason, with the handle itself falling into my lap. If I lost the handle from then on I would be locked in. This is just a small example of the sort of minor incidents that cumulatively start to undermine one's faith in the ability of the car to hold together until journey's end. Fortunately we encountered a second uneventful day as far as the travelling was concerned. The 300 miles were completed without incident as we drove into Lenin Square in the centre of Tyumen at 9 p.m., dead on schedule. We were just so pleased that we were eating up these miles. Even at this stage I felt that I had seen enough of Siberia and I just wanted to get across to spend time in China – but our luck was not to hold out for much longer.

It was hot in Tyumen even at that time of night and the temperature in the car itself had been over 100 degrees for most of the day. I always arrived in a complete sweat. Luckily, on this occasion, there was a freshwater pump in the square so I immediately downed several glasses of water after first putting them through the purifier. We had got into the habit of using the purifier each time we drank and I am convinced that this saved us a lot of problems. The three young men who met us took us to our $80 a night hotel. It is amazing how rates varied so much.

Our hosts were typical of the *nouveau riche* set in Russia. They took us out for a meal that evening and we ended up in a sort of nightclub with folk dancing. The food was good and wholesome and as we were starving I don't think I had eaten so heartily for a long time. I had a fish dish which was delicious and downed a couple of pints of excellent cold beer. We talked a lot about the 'new Russia' and the opportunities it presented to those with a bit of energy and a few ideas. Clearly we were speaking to young men in their early twenties who had seen their parents live a very hard life. They, themselves, had benefited enormously from the new climate and had clearly made a lot of money in comparison to the rest of their local peer group. They said there was no way that Russia could slip back into the old communist-style system of central planning with no room for initiative (or the making of profits) at the local level. Mind you, for every person we met who also expressed an enthusiasm for the new order, there were several more, usually of the older generation, who had lost what little they had had with this change of system and looked back, somewhat wistfully, to the old days. Their lives had always been pretty drab but at least the state had guaranteed a flat, a basic pension and enough food. There had been a certainty about their lives which had now disappeared. The presidential election between the incumbent Boris Yeltsin and the communist leader Mr Zuganov was to take place in the next few days and it would be interesting to see the result, we thought. As well as the general division of thinking between the older and younger generations, we also found that the further east we travelled, the more conservative the population became.

Tyumen appeared to be a very attractive town and was in stark contrast to Chelyabinsk just nine hours behind us. Another feature we found as we travelled further east was that the local areas became increasingly independent from Moscow. It seemed that each area had its own local bosses and retained a good percentage of locally raised revenue, to spend as they chose.

The boys, for that is really what they were, asked us how we had fared so far given the problems for road travellers these days. Apparently we had just crossed one of the most notorious stretches of road, fortunately without incident. Perhaps if we were to have a couple of good travelling days free of mechanical problems then it was as well to have them as we crossed the infamous and dangerous stretches. Now that we were actually on our way and were becoming familiar with the scenery I no longer found myself constantly thinking of the possible dangers that might befall us. But, as I considered these thoughts, I had little idea of what lay ahead just a couple of days hence!

I encountered one custom in Tyumen that I had never seen before, despite the fact that it is, apparently, evident right across Russia. This is the practice of standing at the side of the road with thumbs outstretched as though one was hailing a taxi. The difference is that with everyone trying to make a few extra dollars it takes only a few seconds for a private car to stop and take you to your destination.

We got back to the hotel and made a call to Moscow to state our ETA at the next destination, which was Omsk. I got to bed in the small hours again but felt great. We were now making good progress. I had been fed and watered.

I was having a fascinating time meeting a wide range of interesting people in environments that were so different from those at home. I was at peace with the world and drifted off into a deep sleep.

We took a bit of time the next morning to have a look round the city. We were always in two minds in this respect. We were unlikely ever to come to that part of the world again so it made sense to explore a little whilst we were there. On the other hand, with most Soviet cities being nothing to write home about and given that we had long distances to cover each day, there was always the encouragement to be on our way as soon as possible.

We left Tyumen at 10.30 a.m. and set off on our 400-mile journey for Omsk. There was going to be another time zone change so we put the clocks on an hour before we even set off. It's a pity that we were driving in this direction, I thought. If we had been coming from the east we would have had an extra hour's daylight every few days, which would have made a noticeable difference to some of these runs.

We drove through a very heavy thunderstorm with dramatic flashes of lightning. It was quite a scene. Our Healey, as with all Healeys, leaked at the best of times. During the thunderstorm we were absolutely soaked through. Rain was pouring down the inside of the windscreen and around the doors. Still, at least this kept us cool for a change.

The landscape in this part of Siberia was very flat. Trees everywhere. The Siberian region accounts for 20 per cent of all the world's trees. I think that, by the time we had finished, we had become acquainted with most of them!

The area abounds in wildlife. Luckily, I suppose, we didn't see a bear but we did see deer, squirrels and foxes and plenty of different species of birds of prey. We also saw cowboys. Quite literally, men on horseback looking after large herds of cows. Sometimes, the herds were mixed to include goats and sheep.

We stopped at a roadside café. Again it was similar to the ones we had seen all along. These places were in evidence only about every 150 miles or so. We therefore tended to take the opportunity to stop each time we saw one, even if only to get some fresh tea. When we ate we always had a choice of food. The trouble was that it was always the same choice: meatballs in dough with mayonnaise or meatballs in dough without mayonnaise! At least we could get good-quality vodka quite cheaply and there was always an abundant supply of bread.

We were soon on our way again and discussed whether, on the following day, we would be wise to try and make Novosibirsk in 'one hit'. The name 'Novosibirsk' simply means new (Novo) Siberia (Sibirsk). I am afraid I can't resist showing off the tiny amount of Russian that I know! Novosibirsk was psychologically important. It was the largest city that we would encounter on our journey from Moscow to the border and we considered it to be the halfway stage. We planned to stop there for a couple of days' rest and recuperation. We wanted to stretch our legs and look around a bit. In addition, our map showed that cities were getting a little harder to come by the further east we travelled. There appeared to be little in the way of serious habitation between Omsk and Novosibirsk. The snag was that this would be a long journey. I estimated that it was 450 miles and, as usual, we had no idea of the road conditions.

We were running a little late by now, and I was expecting to reach Omsk by 10 p.m. We had originally advised that we would be there between 8 and 9 p.m. We had arranged, through Victoria back in Moscow, to be met at the police checkpoint. It is worth mentioning here that we encountered police checkpoints every couple of hundred miles or so. They were also evident on every arterial road in or out of major cities. They stopped all suspicious traffic. Of course, with our car being so unusual and the police having little to occupy them, we were *always* flagged down. The police on these internal checkpoints were unfailingly friendly and just curious to know what we were doing. It is fair to say that our car stood out a mile as compared to the normal traffic on the roads. We could not afford to appear unfriendly ourselves at these stops as the police would be more likely to detain us further. We were usually held up for about half an hour as they each took turns to sit in the driving seat and then wanted their photographs taken. I had a Polaroid camera with me and this never failed to impress as we were able to show them a photograph of themselves with the car in a matter of minutes.

Already at this point in our journey it was rare to see a car in these long stretches between the townships. The traffic, such as it was, consisted of heavy vehicles, usually lorries. Most, by now, had very high wheelbases and were getting to the stage where we could almost drive right underneath them without being scathed. Was this an indication of the state of the roads to come, I wondered?

When we arrived at the police cordon for Omsk we were told to wait for half an hour. We really couldn't see why. Had we infringed some rule? Was there a problem? We received a torrent of Russian in reply to our questions but not one scrap could we understand. I was comforted by the fact that the attitude of the police was in no way confrontational. In about 45 minutes all became clear. Out of the mist loomed a very large black Mercedes car. Inside was Ludvil, our contact. Victoria, the night before in our regular Moscow telephone call had given his name to us. The police saluted Ludvil, so clearly he was a man who wielded a lot of influence around here. After a few brief friendly exchanges he drove ahead of us, thus escorting us to our Omsk hotel. We certainly felt comforted, so far at least, that our various city mentors were influential people in their own region. Hopefully this reduced the chances of us finding ourselves in serious trouble.

At the hotel we tried, but failed, to send three faxes to the UK. Communication was now generally difficult, even in the big city hotels. We didn't get to bed until after 2 a.m.

As I drifted off to sleep I reflected on our Siberian crossing so far. For some reason my mind was drawn back to my youth, when I remember seeing an old British-made spy film. It must have been particularly old because it was produced in black and white, but the lack of colour, if anything, seemed to add to the air of mystery. Our hero had been travelling by train for hours, perhaps days, across the Balkans. The train jerked to a stop. Nothing could be seen through the carriage windows because of the dense mist outside. Suddenly, to the accompaniment of a few bars of sinister music, the mist lifted just long enough to read the station sign: 'Tirana' or 'Sofia' or 'Zagreb'! Then the mist descended again as suddenly as it had lifted and the train lurched forward once more into the gloom, taking our hero with it.

And so it was in Siberia, I thought. We had often been travelling for hours, days even, seeing little in the way of habitation or other travellers. Suddenly we would find ourselves deposited in the middle of a city: 'Omsk' or 'Ufa' or 'Chelyabinsk'. We would mingle with the crowd for a while; a crowd that contained no other foreign faces; a crowd wherein the majority had never and would never set foot outside the city environs into the world outside; a crowd of individuals that would go home in the evening to watch their own black and white TV sets. They would see the news from Moscow and view it with the same mix of concern and detachment as would we in the West. The very names of Omsk, Ufa and Chelyabinsk conjured up in my mind's eye, just like the Balkan cities in my youth, a sinister aura of mystery, kindled, no doubt, by my upbringing during the cold war years.

Never before had I been on a journey where the sum of the parts didn't seem to make the whole, where I couldn't mentally link up our various stopovers to form the complete jigsaw of our journey. Instead, like the spy remembered from my childhood days, we would travel through great voids of nothingness for hours on end. Then the fog would clear and we would suddenly be part of a seething mass of humanity – lost in its own insular world. Then, in no time at all, we'd leave this unique world to its own devices and

Will it all fit in?

Bon voyage!

Petrol stop

Moscow - children's home

Petrol stop

M53

Motorway service station

Novosibirsk flat

M53 - a good stretch

M53 detour

Petrol stop

Siberian ditch

M53

M53 quicker to walk

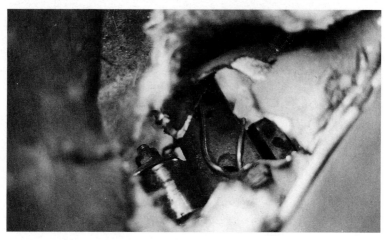

Shattered floor pan, revealing brake pipe

Alexi and Father, Siberian repairs

Exhaust pipe welding - Siberian style

Emerging from the mud - Chichiha

Chinese village school photograph

Junior classroom, village school, Northern Province

Tiananmen Square victory lap!

head off again into the gloomy depths of the next section of crushing nothingness.

Tuesday, 11 June, was a day that shall be etched in my memory for a long time. After four hours' sleep we woke to face what would be a long day in any event. We needed to travel from Omsk to Novosibirsk – a distance of 450 miles – and had decided there was little alternative other than to make it in one go. Our plans were thwarted a few moments later when we were checking out at the foyer. We were advised by a group of lorry drivers that the Novosibirsk road was virtually impassable. There was a 100 mile stretch which was 'under repair'. We had heard this euphemism before. It could mean anything from totally impassable because stretches simply did not exist, to difficult in places but nevertheless possible given enough time. Time was something we did not have in abundance that day. On the other hand, we were told that some of the really big vehicles were getting through. Of course, if there had been an 'AA road watch' broadcast on the radio, or even a telephone number to call for advice on road conditions, then it would be easier to make a decision. This was always our problem: having to make a decision without having full knowledge of the facts. Nobody at the hotel, or elsewhere in the city, knew what road conditions to the next city were like. This was because nobody travelled there. An amazing contrast to life in England. Yet again nobody could even tell us whether there was a time change between the two cities. Remember that these are neighbouring cities, not only in the same country but also in the same 'state'. If it hadn't been for the coincidence that we met the drivers of a passing convoy of lorries, we would never have been advised of the problem.

We had one alternative. This was to take a southern detour and thus miss the bad road. There were two snags. The first was that the total distance would then be 600 miles – way above our expected 'norm'. Secondly, that we would have to pass through a corner of Kazakhstan which was now an independent country. For that we were advised that we would need a visa, which was only available in person from the nearest consular office. In this case it would be in Moscow, about a week's journey back. What a dilemma!

A couple of phone calls to friends by the very helpful hotel receptionist came up with the view that we should be able to cross the border if we explained the situation and stressed our 'charity run' factor. That swayed it and off we went.

After a couple of hours I told Nawal that, according to the GPS we were already in Kazakhstan. He didn't believe it because there had been no border post whatsoever. After a further 30 or so miles we both began to believe it. So much for the necessity to obtain a visa! We just hoped we could get out on the eastern side without problems. Our relatively brief journey through Kazakhstan was totally uneventful. So plain was the scenery that I can't think of a single feature of the terrain, or of the very few places of habitation that we came across, that is worth recounting. However, in the distance we did see what we identified as the Altay Mountains. They were in stunning contrast to the more immediate emptiness all around us but we never did get to drive right across them. We came to a border post on our exit but the police guardsmen, having presumably nothing else to do all day long, simply insisted on talking to us for about half an hour. They never asked for papers and, after the customary couple of Polaroid shots taken of them standing next to the car, we were on our way again.

We stopped at a roadside barbecue for a late lunch of unidentified dead meat. It's amazing just what one will eat when very hungry! A few miles further on we began to slide sideways in the mud and came to rest, precariously, on the edge of a 6-foot-deep ditch. We couldn't move the car by hand, nor could we start the engine again for fear of slipping straight down. Luckily a lorry came past only a few moments later. It stopped and the three-man crew gave us a tow out on to the road again. We always found that there was a great deal of camaraderie between road users. A bit like the sailors at sea, I assume, all sharing the same potential dangers and not knowing when they may need help themselves. A bit different to the reaction you expect if you break down on one of Britain's congested motorways – not a bit of help until the next police car comes along, everyone else is just angry that you are blocking their particular path! We were on our way again but soon discovered that the brakes were not working at all – at least not the foot brake. We had lost all our brake fluid somehow. This was just typical of the sort of incident that was unique to a trip like this in that there was absolutely no chance of calling an expert mechanic to solve the problem – we simply had to sort it out ourselves. The trouble was that it was beginning to get dark at this stage, we still had about 150 miles to go and we were in the middle of a Siberian forest. What could we do? We briefly considered whether we should spend the night there. The trouble with that was that we would simply wake up the next morning (assuming we survived the night!) in exactly the same fix but much more hungry and tired. There really was no choice. We would just have to press on and hope we didn't meet too much coming the other way – particularly the large lumber lorries which always hogged the centre of the road with lights blazing and gave way to no one.

At this stage we were very tired and therefore, despite the protests coming from the underside of the car every time we hit one of the many large stones strewn in our path, we just put our foot down and drove, very fast, eventually entering the city limit of Novosibirsk. By this time it had gone midnight and we were driving slowly round the gloomily lit outskirts, using our hand brake occasionally to slow down, looking for the centre of the city.

Suddenly a van screeched to a halt in front of us making us stop in our tracks (difficult without proper brakes!). Out jumped half a dozen young men, who surrounded the car. One put his arms through the open side screen of the Healey and grabbed my bag. We had got into a routine, when nearing our destination each day, of packing all valuables such as cameras, loose money, passports and GPS etc. into a single bag. In this way then we would know what to grab when leaving the car for the hotel without having to sort everything out in front of a crowd. I guess we would have to refine this policy in future to avoid incidents like this. Anyway, the bag was tipped out in front of us, with the contents rolling down the bonnet. The 'gang', in a rather aggressive manner, rifled through everything and was particularly interested in a couple of £10 notes, which amused them as they showed a picture of the Queen. After a few minutes and with no inkling of what this was all about, I noticed that one of the men went back to his van. He returned waving a pistol and, shouting loudly in Russian, pointed it at me. I remember thinking rather stupidly, I have just resigned myself to losing the cameras and other valuables but if I get shot as well I really will get mad! Meanwhile Nawal had got out of the car and was conversing with another one of the group. After several more seemingly endless minutes, they all jumped into their van again and drove off, having taken nothing. We really weren't too sure what to make of it.

We learnt the following day that they were probably undercover police agents. Several plain-clothes teams had been doing the rounds at night in order to try and combat the rising violent crime rates. They were specifically looking for people carrying firearms. I assumed the incident with the pistol was their attempt, being unable to speak English, to ask if we had been carrying anything akin to what he had been waving at me. I just wished he'd been a better actor and therefore been able to get his point across more easily. I had been taking an occasional dose of laxative in order to combat the lack of fruit or roughage (or pretty well everything else!) in our diet. That was one night where it was not required! We got to the hotel and then to bed at 2.30 a.m. What a day!

The next day was a Wednesday. I felt pretty relaxed for a change because we were going to spend a couple of days in Novosibirsk. Although I was keen to complete the Russian segment of our trip as quickly as possible, I think we were both at the stage where a respite from driving would do us good. The room facilities were adequate for me to have a relaxing bath. This was not always the case. I found that Russian hygiene, in all but the top international hotels, often left a great deal to be desired. The 'baths' in some of the hotels in which we stayed were little more than over-sized zinc basins with rust and assorted scum around the edges. The water was often a deep sludgy brown. In Novo-sibirsk this was not the case and it was a real treat just to unwind for half an hour in hot water.

We found out that it was a national holiday, which was a bit frustrating because it meant that we couldn't get any-thing done. We had wanted a mechanic to look over the exhaust (again!) and to repair the brake system, but this was not to be. Our local contact, Karina Piankhova, was going to go out for the day so we would not meet her. The interpreter who was going to accompany us during the afternoon could not be contacted because only Victoria Ushakova in Moscow had her phone number and, despite repeated efforts, we had been unable to put a call through to Victoria. Maybe it was a good thing to be forced to concentrate on the local scenery for a change. After all, I wanted to get as much out of this trip as I could. This was not a race. We had had certain deadlines to meet in the early stages of our trip due to the close proximity of our sponsors and the need to confirm press conferences several days in advance. As soon as we left Moscow, however, although we had agreed to a couple more press conferences en route, namely in Novosibirsk and earlier in Chelyabinsk, these could be arranged a couple of days beforehand through Victoria, to whom we could give our ETA at each of these cities. Our next major event was to be the crossing of the Sino-Soviet border. We had given Cadbury's China an estimated date for our arrival there but had suggested a couple of days' leeway either side. We planned to finesse this date as we got nearer. We were therefore able to spend a day (or two at a pinch) just sightseeing. It was highly unlikely that I should ever return to any of these Russian cities again, so it made sense to make the most of our stay.

We spent the morning going for a slow stroll towards the centre of the city. It really was a huge place and it was a rather strange experience. Here we were in the middle of a city of perhaps 2 million people. Most of them had never ventured out of the city and its immediate surrounds, let alone out of Siberia. Conversely, very few Westerners had actually visited this city. Here we had a whole mass of people who, in many senses, were cut off from the rest of the world. The ones we met were extremely friendly but their knowledge of England was pretty scant. Surprisingly, given 80 years of communism culminating in 30 years of the cold war, what little they had been taught about England resulted in them, generally, being highly respectful of the country and of the English people as a nation.

At lunch in a café we met the first non-Russians that we had seen since we left Moscow. They were two American girls who were backpacking around Siberia. Similarly, they told us that we were the first non-Russians they had met in the two weeks of their travels so far.

We tried to phone our interpreter again but didn't have any change. The café proprietor was quite happy to provide the necessary coins. Only a small matter, I know, but another example of the friendly and helpful nature of the 'natives' that we met. We made contact at last and after a 30-minute wait Maria, our interpreter, appeared at the café. She was a youngish, rather scatter-brained girl. She proved to be the worst driver I have ever met, but, at the same time, an extremely pleasant girl who was keen to show us as much of her city as she could. I like it when people are proud of their home town. It seems to me that, so often in England, it is almost a national pastime to try and knock our own country.

Maria took us, accompanied by many sounds of crunching gears and the occasional scraping of a passing (or parked!) car, to see two Russian Orthodox churches. They were both extremely ornate. Slightly run-down perhaps, but I was surprised that, after 80 years of communist suppression, they remained in such good order. Churchgoing was then becoming popular again but whether that was simply a new fashion following the communist years or a genuine resumption of a more religious life, I did not know.

She took us to see the beautiful river Ob – apparently the world's fifth longest and I'd never heard of it before! She then took us to the local park, where there was a monument dedicated to those who had died in a local nuclear power plant accident and, alongside that, a similar monument to those who had died at Chernobyl. I assume, therefore, that there were a number of nuclear accidents that the Russian authorities had kept hidden from the Western media.

We came back to the hotel at about 6 p.m. and I had a thorough clean-out of the car boot. It was then that I found the two 'missing' envelopes, filled with dollars, hidden under the carpet. They would keep us going for a little longer but, given the high cost of hotel accommodation in particular, I still calculated that we would have run out of money within a week and it was unlikely that we would have made it into China by then. Nawal continued to refuse to discuss the matter, simply saying that that was my problem.

Maria and her husband rejoined us that evening for dinner. We had a very interesting discussion about the changes in Russia and it was certainly their view that the changes were very much for the better. If I can generalise on this aspect at all, it seemed to me that those below about 40 years of age remained pleased to have seen the end of the communists and their regime. It was a more mixed bag of responses that we heard from the older generation.

To round off the evening we took a stroll around the large park in the centre of the city. There were many people about, all celebrating Independence Day. I never did find out who they were now independent from as I had thought that Russia had never been fully occupied. Despite all the differences in language, culture, politics, religion and history, we found people enjoying themselves in exactly the same way that they do all round the world. There were many family groups walking about or playing on slides and swings. There were people eating hamburgers and drinking Coca-Cola – or at least the Russian equivalent. There were pop bands playing on makeshift stages. Some schools had put on a bit of a show with musical concerts. It was a colourful scene.

The next day it rained solidly. I tried to clean the car but there were bits of tar on the exterior which were virtually impossible to remove. I spent a steady three hours on it. I had changed, I reflected. I don't think I had cleaned a car by hand since I was a teenager. As I was doing this I was reckoning that a three-day stay in Novosibirsk would cost us about $500, which accounted for half of our remaining cash. Nawal had his credit card with him and this was one of the few hotels we had encountered that would take credit cards. How much simpler to pay the bill by this method leaving us with sufficient cash for what I estimated was to be another nine days in Russia. Yet I knew that this was something that Nawal would not agree to.

I was rather pleased with myself in the way that I had changed. I had become more relaxed and more philosophical. Instead of immediately launching into the subject, I thought that I would broach it later that afternoon after, hopefully, a good lunch which would put us both in a good mood. Furthermore, regardless of his response, I would just accept it. I certainly didn't want to have a row about this, despite the logic of my case. The overall objective of getting into China, particularly now that we could almost smell it, was much more important.

Ten minutes later the subject happened to come up naturally in conversation with Nawal and he immediately agreed! Is it me who was becoming more flexible in approach or was Nawal changing his attitude a bit?

We received a phone call from our original Cadbury contact, Karina, who promised to get a mechanic to us, but this would probably not be until 11 a.m. Still, unless there was a major problem with the car, the work should have been completed before our scheduled 5 p.m. press conference. We had been hoping to leave Novosibirsk first thing in the morning.

Although I had phoned home a couple of times I found it awkward to give Jenny a true impression of the trip in the short time available, or indeed to have any meaningful conversation. I found it much better to write a letter spread over a few days and post it at the first opportunity. That afternoon I posted a letter to Jenny and about a dozen postcards to various friends, including those in the Austin Healey Club. The key points could be inserted into the monthly Healey magazine in order for Healey fans to be kept up to date with our adventure.

As the trip wore on we both became increasingly concerned about the state of the car. It really had been taking quite a pounding from the rough conditions of the roads. Neither of us was 100 per cent sure that it would hold together for the duration. As we got ever nearer to China the keener we became just to get over the border and the tenser the atmosphere became as a result.

We were also aware that we still had no confirmation that we had been granted Chinese visas. It would have been a bitter blow indeed if we had got as far as the border but then had to turn back. I had already had my fill of Siberia and we were only halfway. On top of that the logistics of turning round at the Sino-Soviet border were impossible to work out. The car could certainly not have made a return journey. In any case, we would have run out of money by then. Our sponsors would not be prepared to repeat the financing of our reverse passage through their territory. They had already milked us for the maximum commercial benefit. The more I thought about it, the more I realised that we didn't have a contingency plan if we were turned back at the border. What's more, try as I might, I couldn't think of any fall-back plan in that event at all.

I enjoyed another rare spell of privacy for four hours as Nawal, Maria and Karina all went off in the car to the mechanic. I occupied my time by first cashing our remaining dollars into rubles. I then went for another walk but the constant rain made this rather unattractive city seem even more depressing. Uneven road and pavement surfaces, together with lots of dirt and rubble, created pools of dirty water everywhere – even inside the shops. I noticed that even the seasoned locals were regularly sprayed by passing lorries as they drove through deep puddles at top speed.

I bought a picnic lunch in readiness for our journey the next day. This was rather complicated because each item was bought separately. There were no supermarkets in the Western sense. You couldn't just choose items, put them in your basket and pay for everything at the end. Each little section of the food store was the domain of one particular assistant or another who guarded their patch jealously as though expecting another assistant to come along at any moment and wrest it from them. Not knowing the language to any extent I found that I had to point to each item and somehow get across the quantity that I required. This took ages. Then I was issued with a little scribbled piece of paper. I took this to a central desk, miles away, and joined the long queue. Often the paper did not seem to describe my purchase and I was asked questions. This was particularly difficult because I was no longer close enough to point to the item I required. I was treated as though I was a complete imbecile. Eventually I paid for the ticket and returned clutching a different coloured ticket, to where I (hopefully) remembered I had started. I then exchanged the ticket for the item in question but, at this point, there was a great deal of scrutiny to ensure that the numbers matched up exactly with the numbers left on the two eggs or stale bun or whatever it was that I had selected. Only then was I grudgingly allowed to place my purchase in my basket. How a busy mother could possibly shop for a large family with this system in place, I had no idea.

After some considerable time I made my exit from the store clutching my spoils of a large bottle of mineral water, some grape juice, cheese, oranges, apples, bananas, bread and – as a special treat – a large bag of crisps. I trudged back to the hotel through the rain and, in the seclusion of my hotel room, opened a half-bottle of whisky and had a good long slug plus a few crisps. Wow! I had brought the whisky all the way from England and I can't think why I hadn't tasted any until then. It was just what I needed to revive the spirits after a damp and uncertain day. After that I enjoyed a bath and a shave. I washed my clothes and put on a clean shirt and reasonably clean trousers. I felt like a new man. I went downstairs to the hotel lobby and tried to buy some more batteries for the GPS machine – to no avail. I did have a rather good lunch consisting of chicken Kiev (rather apt, I thought) and beer.

Nawal returned, with repaired car, at about 4.30 p.m. The brake problem was, as we had come to suspect, a fractured brake pipe. This had been replaced with a length of brake piping from a Russian fighter plane – the mechanic worked as an engineer at the local military airport! The big problem was that Nawal, on his exit from the garage, had driven straight over an exposed boulder and re-ruptured the exhaust. Silly clot – but too late to do much about it other than to put on our last remaining patch. By the time we had completed this final adjustment we were overdue for our 5 p.m. press conference. As I raced off in a press car with Nawal following, I heard a loud bang behind. The Healey had suffered its first (and only) puncture! We stopped at the side of the main road to change the tyre and arrived hot, sweaty, dirty and late. Just the right frame of mind to embark upon a press conference!

Fortunately the conference was held in a studio filled with communication facilities. Because of our cash shortage it was useful to be offered the use of a phone to call home. I spoke to my eldest son Daniel and he told me that everyone else in the family had gone to watch the Stella Artois tennis championship held at Queen's Club in London. I had been to that tournament many times myself and it seemed such a different world, sitting there in the middle of a remote city, thinking of familiar situations at home. I also found that speaking to just one person at home meant that I could actually have a sensible conversation for a change over the typical three-minute period allowed. My problem with earlier calls had been that I would say the usual preliminaries such as 'How are things?', 'What's the weather like?', 'Any problems at home?' etc. but, just before I was able to develop a proper conversation, another of my children, or perhaps a friend who happened to be in the house at the time, would be put on the line just to hear someone speaking from Siberia. The result was that all my previous conversations were pretty meaningless as I never got past the small-talk stage. Daniel let me know that all was indeed well and that everyone at home was following us on the map, including the children at the local school, as they were being contacted by Cadbury's in Birmingham every few days. We had still been able to get messages through to Cadbury's Moscow via the local agents that we met and these messages were generally being passed back to Birmingham for onward transmission to various interested parties. Daniel said that everyone felt we were making good progress. I guess we were in the sense that we had already got further than some people thought we might. After all I have been on other Austin Healey outings to France, for example, where half the cars break down before they even get to Dover! On the other hand I was concerned that our pace had been slower than hoped. We had had to make too many forced stops. It was clear that we were wrong not to have fitted a rally exhaust, because exhaust problems were the cause of many of our delays. We needed to leave early the following day because the inter-city distances were getting greater and people were telling us that the road conditions would get progressively worse. However, we now needed to repair the puncture as well as the exhaust before we departed, and I just knew that that would take longer than expected.

We left the conference and headed back, in the rain, for the hotel. I had a couple of large vodkas and felt much better. And so to bed.

The Friday proved to be a very frustrating day. We were up, breakfasted and packed by 8 a.m. and were then collected by Maria. She took us to the local Cadbury office, where Nawal gave a talk to the assembled workforce on the art of salesmanship. In the meantime I composed and forwarded a fax to Chris Capstick in Birmingham with our latest news.

At last we were accompanied to a local garage, where our vital repairs were started. I think a word on garages would be useful. I use this general description but a Siberian garage is not at all similar to its namesake in the UK. The garage we went to was little more than a backyard. It looked rather like a small version of a scrap heap with rusted and broken vehicles sprawled everywhere. In the corner was a wooden shed with a pit. That was it! That is not to say that the mechanics were not skilled. They had to be in order to keep most of their own vehicles on the road and, as ours was in reality of a similar age and of a basic design, they were able to work on it. However, problem after problem occurred and what we hoped would take a couple of hours' work dragged on and on throughout the day. At 8.30 that evening I found myself back at the Cadbury office scrounging my first bite as I had not eaten all day. Clearly we were going nowhere that day after all. To make matters worse, when I eventually got through to Victoria in Moscow to explain our latest timing it was clear that we had got our wires crossed earlier. She told me that our next contact in Kemerovo had already been waiting at the police checkpoint for six hours! Apologies all round. I assumed the car would be completed that night and that, perhaps, we could make it all the way to Krasnoyarsk the next day, a distance of 500 miles. But that was not to be. In the meantime we had a more urgent problem – where were we going to sleep that night?

Nawal returned with the car at about 9 p.m. The mechanics had welded a steel sheet along the length of the exhaust pipe to give added protection. The trouble was that this lowered the clearance even further. We discussed the problem of carrying excessive weight and decided to redistribute our load. This meant carrying even more in the car with us in order to reduce the concentration of weight on the back axle. Unfortunately, of course, this led to even more cramped conditions in the cockpit.

Maria very kindly suggested that we could stay at her parents' flat for the night. Yet another example of human kindness. Her parents had what I imagine is a typical Russian flat: very small, spartanly furnished with old-fashioned furniture and with the obligatory rug hanging the length of the living room wall. We used our sleeping bags for the first time, but at least this was in the comfort of someone's living room and not in the wild. We were given a breakfast in the morning and then collected by Maria. The frustration continued as she was an hour late and then, as she drove us off to collect the Healey from its parking spot, got stuck in the mud. Eventually we reached our car but realised the petrol tank was empty and we didn't want to risk leaving the city without a full tank. So back we went into the heavy city traffic to reach a station where they had 95 octane. We eventually left Novosibirsk at midday.

Twenty miles out of town and the exhaust blew again. It must have been knocked just ahead of the silencer box. Yet another delay as we stopped and went through our well-worn routine. Off with the tyre restraining strap on the boot, then the padlock and chain, then we unravelled the groundsheet and then undid the two spare tyres. All our remaining exhaust patches had been used the day before so we simply did what we could to adjust the many jubilee clips that were decorating the pipe and used up the last of our sealer. One hour later we were on our way again with the exhaust still blowing! After a few miles we had had enough of the noise so we stopped again to try and do the job properly this time. All this was very good for my patience. Indeed, I did find myself getting very philosophical about these matters. A few weeks earlier I would have become extremely frustrated and cross but by this time I really did take the attitude that it would take as long as it took. There was nothing more we could do to speed up the process. I did find myself remaining very calm. Not one of my normal traits!

At 2 p.m. we set off again, with little hope in my mind of reaching Krasnoyarsk that day unless we travelled well into the small hours, which was not advisable. Even then it would assume a continuation of good road surfaces and no further problems with the car. Recent history should have suggested that neither of these conditions was likely to last.

We were on tenterhooks every time the car hit a stone – which was every few minutes. However, with no further incidents we made it to Kemerovo by 5 p.m. I was quite keen to press on but Nawal was tired and it would mean driving in the dark for several hours. Kemerovo was not much to write home about but if we pressed on there was absolutely no habitation, according to the map, before we hit Krasnoyarsk. We would be fully committed.

As it happened we were greeted at the Kemerovo police checkpoint with a sign which said in English 'WCE 132 wait here 30 minutes'. There was a lot of confusion as we tried to explain that this was probably meant for yesterday and that these arrangements had now been cancelled. We made a number of phone calls including one to our original local contact, Andreev, who was keen to come out and meet us there and then. We felt we had little choice at this stage other than to stay. We spent the next half-hour or so tightening up bolts and generally tinkering with the car. Andreev, a young man in his twenties, appeared and escorted us back to his flat in the centre of the town and gave us a meal of pizza and beer.

Both Nawal and I felt pretty tired at this stage but we went out for a walk with Andreev and soon revived. Kemerovo was much larger than I had anticipated. It was, and is, a coal-mining town. Strange, therefore, that it was one of the most attractive cities that we had seen in Siberia. Unlike many other cities, the various buildings were not identical to one another. The local architects and builders had also been liberal with the use of colour. By contrast I don't think anyone in Novosibirsk had ever considered erecting a building that was not grey.

We had a good look round the centre and were then taken to a cinema. We were ushered through the cavernous foyer and into a smaller room at the back. Andreev showed a pass to a couple of guards complete with handguns, of course (we were getting used to this), and we were taken upstairs. Here we found about a couple of dozen tables arranged around a small stage. We were offered delicious snacks and plenty of vodka. It was clear we were about to see a show – but what a show it turned out to be! Andreev knew the manager and the choreographer of the show very well and they both sat at our table and talked to us. I assumed, yet again, that Andreev was another 'mafioso' type. He was only in his twenties but he seemed to have got the measure of who wielded the power in this particular region. I imagined that he was another one who had grabbed the opportunity to become an entrepreneur in the post-Soviet era and, so far at least, things had gone well for him. I never really got to know exactly what he did for a living. The show was a very professional striptease performance. The girls were extremely attractive (or was it just that I had spent too long staring at Nawal?) and everything was very tastefully done. It was an unexpected evening's entertainment, particularly given the remoteness of this mining city. But, as I realised, even though it was remote for me, for thousands, possibly millions of people, this was their home town. They liked to enjoy themselves in the same ways as did everybody else in the world. I presume this particular form of entertainment was open only to the small percentage of the population who had money to spare, but in a city as large as this that number must still run into the hundreds. We got back to Andreev's flat at 3 a.m. and I had a good night's sleep.

Next morning we left reasonably early in an attempt to reach Krasnoyarsk. For a change the car was running very well, even though there was the occasional rumble signalling that we still had a slight fracture in the exhaust. Being the optimist, I was expecting to reach our destination by early evening.

As we went along the road, conditions worsened. We were beginning to learn a few tricks of the trade. For example, if we hit an unexpected bump then by swiftly rocking the steering wheel from side to side it gave us a better chance of landing on all four wheels simultaneously. This limited the strain on the front axle. We also found that our better weight distribution allowed us to travel an extra 10 m.p.h. on average. On the good stretches we were now able to cruise at about 50 m.p.h. We had emptied our jerrycans because we reckoned we would find adequate petrol supplies for the time being and weight considerations were now the more important factor. However, we held on to the empty cans just in case the situation changed a couple of days further along the route.

We discussed the difficult problem of being unable to get accurate information about the route ahead of time. It was so difficult to plan timings or alternative routes should conditions be too bad. We were still working on the basis that roads were reasonable as far as Irkutsk. 'Reasonable' is, of course, a relative term. In this case it meant no boulders more than 6 inches high to be strewn across the road more frequently than every 500 yards. Even with this definition, there were very many lengthy stretches of 'unreasonable' roads. We soon learnt the Russian for bad: *plokha*. The number of times we groaned when we heard the expression 'road very *plokha*'! We still hadn't yet heard anyone voice an opinion as to the state of the terrain east of Irkutsk. I was more and more convinced that Irkutsk marked the end of the known world!

Pulling up at one of the now rare roadside cafés, we ate a kebab and bread with tea and vodka. It cost $2. As usual, about a dozen people appeared from nowhere. In the villages the children just couldn't believe the sight as we drove past. There were high-pitched shouts as they called to their friends to come and watch. The universal thumbs-up sign was in evidence everywhere we went. With 200 miles to go I was now estimating a slightly later ETA in Krasnoyarsk of 8 p.m. providing there were no further problems. Unfortunately there were!

We sometimes talked about the image that people at home had of our journey. Perhaps some felt that we were lapping up the miles on an exciting adventure with just the occasional hiccup. It really seemed to me, however, to have been very much more of an endurance test. Every mile seemed to be a challenge. I really got to know every nut and bolt on that car and felt for each one as we lurched ever forwards. We stopped for petrol just 100 miles short of our destination. When we tried to start her up again the engine was dead. The alarm system would not deactivate. What could we do? I unpacked the boot for perhaps the tenth time that day and got out the manuals. We realised that we were carrying nothing which would describe the detail of the alarm system. We decided to try and drill it out but first needed to disconnect it from the battery without knowing which were the relevant wires. We took a guess, which proved, luckily, to be correct. This whole episode was yet another lengthy delay to our plans. It took almost two hours, during which time I received a nasty burn on my forearm from the exhaust pipe. I thought I knew every twist in that pipe intimately by now, but it still managed to catch me unawares.

At 7 p.m. we left the station, with 100 miles to go. Half a mile up the road, on the outskirts of a town, we managed to rip the exhaust right off the car – quite literally. There was a dreadful wrenching sound and as we looked back there was the whole exhaust system lying in the sand and gravel which made up that particular stretch of road. A car containing three youths stopped and spent a great deal of time trying to help us. Another driver stopped and tried, unsuccessfully, to explain something to us. He then disappeared. Half an hour later he reappeared with a clamp that he had just constructed back at his home. We managed to get the system roughly back together and by 10 p.m. were

106

off again, only for the same thing to happen a mile further on!

We limped on with a noise that would have woken the dead and shortly reached a police station. We were a little concerned because we had been repeatedly warned in Kemerovo that our next stretch of road was another notorious area for armed robbery. It didn't help that we were struggling along in the pitch-dark, drawing a great deal of attention to ourselves. The police were also concerned for us and I noticed that they were all heavily armed. We had got to the stage where we accepted handguns as a matter of course but these boys were also equipped with machineguns! We made a phone call ahead to our given contact name in Krasnoyarsk advising them that we were unlikely to see them that night. We didn't know whether to bed down in the police compound or push ahead. We decided to go on regardless. I can't remember why because, looking back on the situation, it would have been far safer to stay where we were. However, I guess that what swayed the argument was the fact that there was no food and, moreover, we would be facing exactly the same problem in the morning yet would still be miles from any mechanical help. We eventually limped in to the Krasnoyarsk police checkpoint at 3.30 a.m. Yet again the locals showed kindness on two counts. Firstly, a motorist who happened to be leaving the city took the trouble to turn around and lead us directly to our hotel a couple of miles further on. Secondly, when we checked in and explained the nature of our trip, the receptionist immediately reduced the room rate from 400,000 rubles to 220,000 – nearly 50 per cent discount! Bed this time at 4 a.m.

I woke up on Monday, 17 June seriously wondering if we would ever make it to China. Every mile was now a struggle and we still had 1,000 more to go, having completed about three-quarters of our Trans-Russian segment. Still, I supposed that this meant it was now a lot easier to carry on than it would have been to turn round again. The car seemed to be held together with wire. Every day seemed to bring fresh mechanical concerns and we still had the worst roads to come. I just couldn't think what we would do if we were prevented from crossing into China!

We woke up late and tried, unsuccessfully, to contact Mikhail Velcro, the name given to us by Victoria. She really had been a sweetie. It had certainly made life a lot easier being given the name of a local. They would guide us to our hotel, find a mechanic for us and, we assumed, help us out a little if we got into any trouble, although this last point was yet to be seriously tested. Krasnoyarsk was really the last of the very big Russian cities on our route. We thought, at that stage, that we would be likely to stay there for two days, i.e. three nights.

We received a message from Mikhail that he would be calling for us in the early afternoon, so with a little time on our hands we went out to look over the car. We found that, unbeknown to us, the rear wheel had been damaged and this had had a knock-on effect on the tyre as well. So, out again with all the tools from the boot. This really was becoming a wearying process, I thought. We changed the wheel and thought that at least as we were about to go to the local garage, this was as good a time as any to discover something else that needed attention.

As we were working on the car in an open car park we were observed by someone who came over and asked us to come across to his office. He was very interested in what we were trying to achieve. He was also keen to look at our proposed route. I can't think why because it seemed to me that from this point on, if we were travelling east then there was no alternative at all. However, I guessed that he just hadn't heard of too many people, at least in a private car, driving in that direction. He advised us that the route as far as Irkutsk was reasonable. However, he also said that 'as far as he knew' it wasn't too bad for the next leg from Irkutsk to Ulan-Ude. This was the first time anyone had mentioned any possibility of travel beyond Irkutsk. He may have been wrong about the road condition, of course, but it gave me encouragement that at last someone had admitted that at least there was a road of sorts thereafter! Unfortunately he went on to say that the 'final' two legs after that of approximately 300 miles each, would be over very bad roads indeed. For a Russian to say 'very bad' was in itself very bad!

I think that it was as a result of this conversation that we first considered the alternative of putting the car on a lorry until we had crossed the border. We weren't too sure if this would be considered cheating but we were both getting increasingly concerned that the car might simply disintegrate with any further pounding. At least, if we could find a friendly lorry driver and grease his palms with rubles, then we would preserve the car in readiness for the final 1,500 miles through China. Now that we had got this far it would be a shame if the car just 'died' before we had crossed the border. We were both really looking forward to driving through China. An alternative thought was simply to unbolt the exhaust, kit ourselves out with earplugs and then drive to the border. We could re-bolt the exhaust once across.

Mikhail and Victor, the interpreter, proved to be very affable people. They took us to a garage, where we hung about for quite some time supervising repairs. We were also able to collect some more jubilee clips (and there was I thinking we had already cornered the world market – the exhaust pipe itself now resembled the jubilee clip production line!). We also purchased more exhaust bandages. Of course, as well as the extra days' delays that these recurring problems had caused us, they had also accounted for a considerable portion of our travel budget.

We took a couple of hours off from mechanic watching and were taken by our hosts a few miles out of town up the steep road to a vantage point. From there we could see the extensive city of Krasnoyarsk laid out before us and the wide river on which it was founded winding its way up to the Arctic Circle. This was the river Yenisey and is the world's sixth longest, after the river Ob that we had seen a few days earlier in Novosibirsk. It was a breathtaking view. In the distant city we could make out the huge radar station that Eduard Shevardnadze once described as being 'bigger than the Great Pyramid of Egypt'. After returning to our hotel to freshen up, we were taken out to dinner by Mikhail and Victor and I realised that this was the first food that I had eaten all day. One of the many aspects of the trip that amazed me, as one who loves his food, was that the act of eating had really retreated in my mind as a priority. It had become vitally important to ensure that our only means of transport was in as good a condition as possible; everything else had become secondary. Only when we were satisfied on that score would bodily needs be catered for.

The next day, a Tuesday, was a rest day. We enjoyed a good late breakfast together of cold boiled egg, bread, jam, tea and fruit juice – quite a feast!

Nawal got on his high horse after the meal to say, in short, that he had been thinking about the money situation and that it was my responsibility. He felt that I should have been more accurate than I was. He said that I often said things with certainty which later proved incorrect. Actually I hadn't got a clue what he was talking about and to make matters worse he took about half an hour to say it. I felt like pointing out all the misjudgments that he had made. He did feel that he was a very superior being, I thought. On the other hand, I was beginning to understand him more and more. I also felt that I had changed – and for the better too. For example, at that moment, rather out of character, I thought it best simply to listen to this tirade and just nod occasionally. I took the view that he was simply very tense. I thought that he was worried about the continuing pressure on the car and was uncertain about the chances of crossing the border even at that stage. It was his car and he loved it so I expect that he felt under a great deal of pressure at that stage in the journey and was particularly concerned that his 'baby' should survive this ordeal. I suspected that he would like to consider the lorry alternative but that we simply didn't have sufficient cash resources with us for this to be possible and that it was this thinking that sparked off his monologue on my responsibility for the cash. I felt as though he expected me to suddenly produce a couple of thousand US dollars from my back pocket or something. I thought back to his earlier conversations about sharing everything but at the same time saying that he had nothing and that I had a lot. What was he really trying to say, I wondered. Yet I said nothing and shortly afterwards he was as friendly as pie.

We had had little sleep and the nearer we got to the border the more acute the tension became. Neither of us really knew what lay around the next corner and it was perfectly understandable that each of us should occasionally let off a bit of steam. In fact it was a surprise to me that these occasions were relatively few. To be fair to Nawal, I do believe that he has many virtues. For example, he showed a strong sense of responsibility and perhaps this was why he sometimes found the pressure of the trip a little too much to bottle up. Indeed, I doubt if I could have succeeded on the trip with anyone other than Nawal. He was very tenacious and that had proved to be a necessary requisite. I also felt that he genuinely thought that he was teaching me a thing or two about how the world works outside the cosseted lifestyles enjoyed in England's south-east. Perhaps he was right.

Indeed I did feel that I had learnt a great deal. I had learnt from Nawal but I had also learnt simply from the conditions that I had found myself in and from the people I had met. I had learnt about myself; what I was capable of under pressure and, conversely, what my limitations were. I had reorganised my priorities. I had learnt a lot about how to handle awkward moments without being able to refer to anyone else. On a trip like this, I felt, one was very much on one's own and it was quite sobering and all very good for the soul.

I also felt that, perhaps, I should have been helping Nawal a lot more with his own life and attitudes. Perhaps I was rather selfish and was solely savouring the various highlights of the trip on the basis of judging how I reacted to them myself. It was all very interesting but Nawal, too, needed advice with some aspects of his life. In my opinion he was a very talented man. But it was almost as though he needed a manager, someone who would help him organise his life much better – organisation being one of his weaker points. If his talents could be channelled in the right direction and a lot of the mundane but necessary aspects of his life better organised, then I thought it would have improved his life immensely. He would have been in a better shape financially and he would have been able to use his time much more effectively to enable him to enjoy the wide range of pursuits in which he had expressed an interest. Maybe I should have taken the lead in these matters and tried to give him some advice.

I record the thoughts above just to show the sorts of things that were passing through my mind. To spend a considerable amount of time thinking about these matters just showed how much one's mind was affected when spending 24 hours a day for several weeks with another person. That one-to-one relationship becomes vitally important, particularly on a trip like this where it was just the two of us against the various elements. And the elements were pretty hostile most of the time. I wondered what on earth it must have been like for the hostages such as Terry Waite, John McCarthy and Brian Keenan. In their case they were bonded together for very much longer. Their situation was so very much more precarious and uncertain. They were never sure if they were about to face death. The mental pressure must have been absolutely crushing.

Mikhail and Victor collected us from the hotel after breakfast and took us back to Mikhail's flat, where we met his wife. Mikhail was a well-educated individual. He was a senior manager of one of the largest businesses in Krasnoyarsk and therefore, we were told, was entitled to rent one of the best flats in the city. But by Western standards this 'superior' flat was tiny and had very little in the way of facilities. This was a hangover from the Soviet days, when in general the standard of life was well below that enjoyed in the West, yet it was cheap and life had a certainty about it. In the modern Russia there was no longer a safety net. If you were a hard-working and/or shrewd individual, then it was now possible to make a lot of money and to raise your living standards appreciably. However, for the mass of people who were unskilled, then no longer could they assume that the state would provide their vital needs of food and shelter, even at a basic level. I could understand why many of the older generation looked on the passing of the Soviet era with mixed feelings.

Our hosts took us out for a sightseeing trip and then we stopped at a roadside barbecue for a meal. Someone had told Mikhail that I could speak French. Apparently this was unusual in this part of the world but his secretary happened to speak French. He had been waiting for the moment to take me to the office so that I could converse with her in this language. The ensuing somewhat basic conversation took place in front of a small crowd of onlookers. I felt as though I was a Martian or something trying to communicate with earthlings for the first time ever, such was the interest shown. I couldn't quite understand it but after about five minutes of this pantomime everyone started to clap so I had obviously passed the test.

We returned to our hotel in the late afternoon and faced an unusually empty few hours – which made a very pleasant interlude. We did try to make contact with Peter Kirby in Moscow as Nawal had hopes of persuading him to sub us for $1,000 to be collected in Irkutsk, which we would repay once we had returned to England. We were also waiting for Victoria to telephone us in order to arrange for our next contact in Irkutsk. We hoped to make the 550-mile journey the next day in one go. The theory was that we would start at 5 a.m. and reach our destination about 7 p.m. I went to bed thinking, why do I know it is not going to be that easy?

We set off the next morning at dawn as planned. I think we were both a little apprehensive. This would be the last of our very long runs. We had 'borrowed' two short planks of wood and strapped them on to the boot of the car. This was our answer to the very bad stretches of road. I would

113

place them over the major potholes for Nawal to drive over. Seemed a good idea at the time but a bit time-consuming to say the least if the potholes went on for a hundred miles or so!

We were about an hour out of Krasnoyarsk when the car started to give off its familiar scraping sounds as the low-slung exhaust repeatedly hit the ground. This was not a good sign. However, we had already passed the first test. Surprisingly, perhaps, city roads were generally worse than the inter-city routes. I think this is because more traffic uses them and they are rarely repaired. It is also because the tram system is still very much in evidence throughout Russia's major cities. The tramlines are frequently laid on top of the road surface creating major problems for us as they are a good 4 inches proud of the surface. Sometimes much more. The planks had already come in handy!

By 3 p.m. we were beginning to struggle. Road conditions were getting steadily worse. We completed a 20-mile stretch where we would have found it easier travelling across the fields alongside, were it not for the hedgerows between the fields. Twenty miles may not sound too far but as we were continuously crawling up and down large ruts it took us a good three hours. I walked most of the way, manhandling the planks. We actually became completely stuck at one point with all four wheels off the ground as the car was suspended on its chassis by a large boulder. We had tried to take a run at it in order to bounce over but we had ground to a halt, unable to get any traction. It took a good half-hour for a lorry to pass by and they then gave us a tow. This slow speed caused other problems. The radiator was constantly boiling over and we had no spare water with us.

This was a region of thick Siberian forests that provided great wealth from the sale of timber. The proceeds were supposed to be distributed to the population as a whole, but in reality largely found their way back to a relatively small number of officials in Moscow, we were told. The whole region was also rich in minerals, particularly coal, oil and gas deposits. Diamonds and gold had also been discovered but not in such quantities in this particular area as to be commercially viable.

We alternated between perhaps 30 miles of smoothish surface then even longer stretches where we just crawled along. It was obvious that we were not going to make it to Irkutsk that night. The final straw occurred when we managed to turn the car right over when going round a corner. This was much more to do with the adverse camber of the road and the muddy conditions at the time than our speed. The Healey came to rest at right angles, with the underside facing the road and my door wedged against the bottom of the roadside ditch. Luckily for us, two lorries were close at the time. They stopped and we were dragged out of the ditch in a matter of minutes. Neither of us had been injured. It had been a very long day and we eventually limped in to the town of Tulun after dark, with exhaust blowing, rear bracket loose, a suspected blown manifold gasket, no front hubcaps, rear luggage rack bolts sheared off, wing mirror shattered and various sundry problems. We drove past a guest house which looked extremely basic but it was the only place in town and it charged only $4 per night. What more could we ask? All rooms were taken but, true to form, the manager kicked everyone out of the television room and we were allowed to kip down on the floor. We weren't allowed to go to sleep for some time, however, because everyone wanted to know more about us. We had a very drunken evening, or should I say early morning, because it was well into the small hours by then. We swapped our life stories with a dozen lorry drivers and a good time was had by all as the one thing in plentiful supply was vodka. It must have been a strange scene.

I remember thinking at the time that this was another very different experience for me, one that few tourists, even to this part of the world, ever experience. It was a bit like an extract from an Indiana Jones film. The mix of characters was fantastic. They included very rough-looking Outer Mongolians in their full gear, headdresses and all, burly Russian truckies looking as though they weighed 25 stones each at least, wily Chinese who were intent on gambling with anyone who cared to name a bet. There was an assortment of Eastern Europeans who were 'only doing this' in order to earn money for their families back home (what did they mean by 'this' I thought – drug-running?) They looked very sly when explaining their business with lots of winks and nudges. There was also a sprinkling of females and most of them looked even tougher than their Russian male counterparts. I was frightened to death of the lot of them.

In the morning I had a little look round the 'motel'. The structure was reminiscent of one of those old holiday bungalows sometimes still found at the English seaside. It was entirely constructed of wood. The toilet facilities were non-existent. I don't know what you were supposed to do about that! The washing facilities consisted of one semi-tiled room with a single cold tap. I waited until the queue had died down a bit and then brushed my teeth and had a cold shower at the same time. One of the little sheds that butted on to the main building was the dining room. It consisted of a counter, behind which stood a fearsome-looking lady, and behind her was a double-ring gas cooker. She gave us eggs and cold meat and some thick bread plus tea. We sat at one of the two Formica tables. Despite these basic conditions, everyone was extremely friendly and tried to help us and talk to us whenever possible.

After breakfast Nawal went to supervise the repairs to the car, which was being worked on in the backyard. I went out to see how work was progressing and was met by a stench from the nearby trees – that solved the problem of the missing lavatory facilities!

One good thing for us about these regions was that everyone had to be self-sufficient. Almost every male was a self-styled mechanic. At a place like this where they were receiving travellers all the time, then there was a ready supply of both willing and able experienced hands who were very happy to spend all their morning, if necessary, just trying to get us back on the road again. Throughout our journey so far we had found a certain camaraderie between travellers including those, such as the motel staff, who came across them regularly.

While Nawal continued to mastermind events in the garage, I went to try and make a telephone call to Irkutsk. Clearly I needed to explain our current predicament and to make some arrangement for being met there. Our system of a series of friendly contacts organised by Victoria way back in Moscow (now nearly 4,000 miles behind us) had started to break down. It had served us very well indeed and I had been pleasantly surprised by just how many contacts she had been able to unearth. Not only that but each one had been only too willing to help us. I had originally thought that she might have come up with a name in two or three key cities east of Moscow but that that would be it. In fact her chain of contacts had been a superb aid to us and had lasted all the way to Krasnoyarsk. However, for the last couple of stopovers, although we had had contacts, these had been arranged as friends of the previous ones. By this stage no one had heard of Cadbury's. They were simply a business associate or a personal friend of our contact in the previous town. That did nothing to diminish the attention and care that they afforded us. In fact we were looked after in all but the two final Siberian destinations – not bad going when you think about it!

The trip was proving a fascinating lesson for me in many ways. For example I was constantly reminded of all those little things that make up the fabric of life as we know it in England, yet take for granted without giving a moment's thought. My telephone call to Irkutsk was one such incident. Irkutsk was, after all, just the next city to the east but a telephone call was not an easy matter to arrange. The motel phone could only reach numbers in Tulun. When I explained to the manager what I wished to do he immediately dropped everything he was doing and took me in his car to the centre of the town. I was taken to an office, which I presume was the town hall, and taken up to the second floor, where I was asked to wait. The manager went in and returned about 15 minutes later, beckoning me to follow. I went through the next door and saw a number of people facing me sitting behind desks at the far end of the large room. The man in the centre was wearing a suit. This was a very unusual sight as we hadn't seen anybody in a suit for some considerable time. Clearly he was the 'big cheese' in this part of the world. He spoke a little English which, again, was somewhat unusual this far east. He said that he understood that I wished to make a call to Irkutsk. He then said that he had been told that we were trying to drive to China and that we were raising money for charity. Was this true? I slowly explained our situation and he nodded. He then reached for the phone and dialled the Irkutsk number. A hush fell on the room as he spoke, obviously in Russian, to the person who answered. After a few moments he handed the phone to me. When I spoke I heard the voice of Vladimir Nikolenko, our contact in Irkutsk, who spoke reasonable English. Slightly disconcerted because the assembled team of about a dozen officials was listening in to my conversation, I explained when I thought we might get to Irkutsk and arranged a rendezvous. I then put the phone down with something of a flourish because the occasion seemed to require a gesture like that. There were smiles all round. I thanked the 'mafioso boss' for his invaluable assistance and asked how much I owed him for the call. He said, 'This is a present from the people of Tulun to you as a charity worker and as a sign of friendship to the English people.' It was, to say the least, a little over the top. Even though I had only made a five-minute phone call to someone in the next town I felt as though I had been present at some sort of major diplomatic coup. I thanked everybody profusely and was driven back to the motel. What a peculiar occasion!

By midday the car was finished. Nawal had had both the sump guard and skid shield unbolted and beaten back into shape before being re-bolted. We would have made much faster time if we had been driving an off-road vehicle with a high wheelbase. On the other hand the Austin Healey was helping to create publicity and this worked well for several reasons, including PR for the charity and for our sponsors. We had heard that a pair of Range Rovers had tried a similar journey the previous year. One had had a mechanical breakdown which could not be repaired on the spot and the other one had been stolen. Perhaps there is no easy way after all!

Our newly made friends at the guest house gave us a marvellous send-off. Perhaps 40 people in all came out to wave us goodbye. Immediately outside the town we had to stop to pull the exhaust pipe up with wire as far as it would go to avoid it scraping along the road surface. A few moments later Nawal thought he could smell burning. Then he felt the clutch slipping. After investigation this proved to be simply a loose rubber on the pedal. We really were getting paranoid!

We had about 180 miles to go, which at a modest average speed of 30 m.p.h. would take six hours. It took us eleven! We reached our hotel at midnight. I was at the stage where I had seen enough of Siberia. Going was tough and therefore very tiring. I was keener than ever just to try and get the car on to a lorry at Irkutsk and unload it at the other side of the border. I decided to make enquiries the next day.

Irkutsk is one of the few spots in eastern Russia that is a tourist magnet. For the first time since Moscow we met several foreigners, including many Americans. A few miles to the east of Irkutsk, just a short coach tour away, lies the magnificent and extensive Lake Baikal. This is the largest lake in the world containing 20 per cent of all the world's fresh water. Many rare species of flora and fauna grow in the vicinity. It was a real beauty spot and the town was more cosmopolitan than anything we had seen before. Of course none of the many visitors that we spoke to had any plans to travel out of the city other than to the lake. Traffic outside these areas remained minimal.

One of our problems was that we still had at least two or three nights left in Russia once we had left Irkutsk. We had food and petrol to buy. We were incurring steady costs for the constant repairs for which we hadn't fully budgeted. I was getting concerned as our liquid funds were dwindling rapidly and there was no easy answer as to how we could rectify our cash-flow problem. We seemed to be cut off from the world: no automatic teller machines or anybody who seemed prepared to give us cash on the back of a credit card or, even, to cash our traveller's cheques. I suppose we felt a little like those who are in a prison. We carried all our personal possessions with us. There was no reserve to tap until we got home again. Every item took on a new 'value'. Just as prisoners use cigarettes as currency, so we too viewed our T-shirts, watches, cassette tapes and the like, more and more as instruments of barter that we might have need of in the immediate days ahead.

I disagreed with Nawal concerning our onward plans. Not only would further road travel from here be damaging, possibly fatal, to the car but, at our rate of progress, would add an extra week or so to the trip. I was already missing home a lot and didn't want to spend forever trudging on through Siberia.

I realised that by now we were both almost constantly exhausted. The occasional good night's sleep did help a lot but we were not eating very much and each day drained us a little more. We both felt better after a good meal in the hotel, with the only distraction being that we were accompanied by a drunk who prattled on about Chechnya and Northern Ireland. I think he was trying to put the entire blame on me, personally, for invading Northern Ireland!

At 3 a.m. I was woken by a phone call from Victoria in Moscow. Here she was, an intelligent and well-educated young lady, and yet she really had no idea that by this stage we were in a time zone seven hours ahead of Moscow. What is there about these people that makes them so insular in their thinking? However, I was delighted to hear from her because she had been such a help to us throughout. She gave us a lot of news. She said she was sorry that she had been unable to give us good contacts for this part of the journey. She told us that the Chinese were expecting us from the 22nd – only two days away. The visa would be ready from the 24th onwards. I couldn't quite work out the reason for a difference in these two dates. As it happened it was more likely that the earliest we would get to the border would be the 24th anyway. I asked Victoria if there was any chance of getting this message back to China because we were finding it impossible now to make outgoing calls. She also said that Radio 5 had broadcast another feature on us based on the reports that we had managed to get out via Cadbury's. They were also trying to arrange a further interview with us.

We spent the day looking round Irkutsk, which was not particularly exciting but it did have a good natural history museum exhibiting the interesting plant and animal varieties that were evident in the area. We were awaiting a further call from Victoria and we also tried to call Beijing direct, but to no avail. I made some enquiries about taking the car on the Trans-Siberian freight train for the next 600 miles to the border but this proved very difficult and expensive so I ruled it out. Nawal had never really been keen on this alternative so I resigned myself to the original idea of a continuous drive and just hoped that the car would hold together.

My minor coup of the day was to talk the hotel manager into cashing a $100 traveller's cheque, which he did out of his own pocket. Pity I couldn't have talked him into cashing $500.

The day finished on a much brighter note. Vladimir, our local contact, called and took us to a very pleasant restaurant for dinner. I think Nawal and I must have worked out all our individual concerns on each other by that stage because we were closer that evening than ever before. We truly relaxed and had an excellent evening. Lots of joking and good humour generally. Vladimir's English was not good after all; in fact it was non-existent. It must have been his interpreter that I talked to on the phone from Tulun. Most of our evening consisted of Nawal and me frantically

121

searching through our various phrase books just to keep our conversation going. It was that that caused a series of silly jokes between us and I think I laughed more that night than I had done since we set out from England several weeks earlier. It was a good release.

On Saturday morning we set off for Ulan-Ude. We really thought we were getting close to China now. We were just 20 miles north of Outer Mongolia and would spend the next few hundred miles travelling eastwards in parallel to its northern border. The features of the locals had changed. Most now had very discernible Mongol or Chinese features. Vladimir, in Irkutsk, had given us the name of a friend of his in Ulan-Ude and had also made a reservation for us at a local hotel. This one even featured in the Lonely Planet guide so it should be reasonable, I thought.

Despite all our concerns regarding the unknown quantity of conditions east of Irkutsk, this proved to be one of our best travelling days for some time. The lack of serious problems for just this one day was enough to make a huge difference to our mood. We had a number of minor mishaps – Nawal sheared off the bracket that held the oil overspill bottle and we couldn't fix it to begin with because we had lost the long tie snaps. However, we burned and then fused two shorter ones together and this seemed to do the trick. We also had two occasions where the exhaust rattle caused us to stop and we went through the whole lengthy routine of undoing all the baggage to get to the boot and find the relevant materials for a repair. But that was getting such a regular routine that we did it automatically.

We travelled along the southern shore of Lake Baikal and then turned north for a few miles up its eastern edge. It was a beautiful sight. We were now quite close to mountains which provided a perfect backdrop. We were further encouraged by the weather, which was sunny without being too hot – just perfect. Strangely, the heat suddenly reminded me of a warning I had been given by a nurse back home. Around eastern Siberia, particularly 'in hot weather near water,' she had said, 'there is a danger of contracting tick-borne encephalitis, which is a very nasty disease indeed.' I had no idea what one was supposed to do to avoid it though so I simply made a conscious decision to try not to attract any ticks and left it at that!

Our spirits were lifted even further when we remembered that breakfast had been included in the room rate at Irkutsk. This was quite unusual as we normally had to pay separately for each piece of toast etc. In this case we had managed to take sufficient food with us for a very acceptable picnic lunch.

I calculated that we were, at least in theory, only two days away from China by this stage and that gave us a great deal of encouragement. Perhaps we were going to make it after all. I suspect that Nawal had never really doubted this.

As we passed through the Ulan-Ude police checkpoint we were flagged down as usual. In fact we had never yet managed to drive past a checkpoint, as most of the other vehicles seemed to be able to do. The police, again with very noticeable Mongol features, were extremely friendly. They were laughing and joking and acted like little children when I brought out my Polaroid. We were able to give them a couple of snaps of them sitting at the wheel of the Healey right there and then.

We had entered the Buryatia region, which contains Russia's largest minority – the Buryats. Buryatia, in truth, extends beyond Russia's boundaries to encompass parts of Mongolia and China. It is a region defined more by the location of its Mongol peoples rather than a specific political or geographically defined area. The capital city of Russian Buryatia is the extraordinary town of Ulan-Ude – where Genghis Khan originated.

We found our hotel with no trouble in this relatively small and very strange town. As we arrived at the front doors, we saw, and heard, a local woman giving a welcome to some visitors from a neighbouring region. This welcome came in the form of a strange high-pitched chant which was eerily attractive. Just sitting there in the warm evening sunshine, surrounded by people with Chinese features, in a town with a most unique architectural mix and which nestled between clearly visible snow-capped mountain peaks, was a moving and unusual experience. Few people had shared this particular atmosphere, I thought to myself.

We were unable to make contact with our local 'agent' but that didn't seem to matter as we had easily found the hotel and, for a change, didn't need the services of a mechanic. We went out for a meal and ordered a cheese omelette and chips. We got two fried eggs, a lump of cheese and, about half an hour later, some boiled potatoes. We took it in our stride. All in all, a very successful day. We planned to make it to Chita on the next day and then, on the day after that, we could be in China. All thoughts of getting a lorry to transport the car were banished. We just hoped the roads would remain reasonable.

I tried again to cash some traveller's cheques the following morning but even the local American Express office, which we discovered, was unable to help. Never mind. We were close to China now and with our spirits soaring at that thought we were the best of pals again and off we went, aiming for Chita by that evening. It was good to be alive!

One thing that Nawal mentioned right at the start, based on his earlier experiences on his 1993 trip to Moscow, was the likelihood that our emotions would rise and fall more acutely than normal. It was true. The good days were brilliant and the difficult days were very depressing indeed. The only thing that mattered to us both was getting across that border. To have this single objective in our minds for the last six weeks was, in a strange way, rather refreshing. It blocked out all our normal concerns. It was a very long time since I had given serious thought to what I should do with the rest of my life now that I had retired. I am sure I had all the usual concerns that most people have, some trivial and some more important, but everything had paled into insignificance over recent weeks. China was the driving force. That is what we had both been concentrating on to the exclusion of everything else. And we were nearly there!

We went through what would be our final time change.

In fact, to be more accurate, this would be the last time we would put our clocks forward by an hour. Even though we would travel even further east when in China, we would, in fact, be putting our clocks *back* by two hours once we crossed the border. This is because, unusually for a large country, the whole of China is in the same time zone. All the clocks are based on Beijing time. This means that those in the eastern cities such as Harbin (close to Vladivostok) have few light evenings, whereas on China's western borders there would be little morning daylight. I suppose this was all down to the communists' ideas of central planning.

Our journey to Chita was somewhat uneventful but we were unable to maintain anything like the average speed that we had been hoping for. As a consequence we arrived just before midnight. We asked the way to the Hotel Dauria, and the two boys in the car that had stopped for us asked us to follow them and said they would lead the way. The hotel was large and rather seedy and the night reception staff unhelpful. However, our floor lady cooked us some frankfurters. Then we went straight to bed, dreaming of China the next day. Little did we realise that we would be faced with two major problems before we eventually got across.

In the morning we debated whether we should wait until 9 a.m., when the post office opened. We had been unable to contact China and we really didn't know what the arrangements were for crossing the border. We certainly weren't carrying any Chinese visas with us. We were also not sure whether they had received our message that we were unable to make it by the 22nd and that the 24th would be our earliest possible arrival date. Unfortunately there were no breakfast facilities in the hotel. When we drove down to the post office, we discovered that they had no international fax or telephone facilities at all. Not a great start to the day. We just had to trust to luck that there would be a message waiting for us at the border and that the Chinese had deduced that our arrival date was bound to be a bit of a moveable feast.

We made slow but steady progress. Petrol was quite scarce at this stage so we stopped as soon as we noticed a petrol tanker at the side of the road. We asked for 93 octane and a bucket was filled from the tanker and poured into the Healey. There was no sign as to the strength of the fuel so, again, we just had to hope that this was OK.

We got very excited as we passed the final 100-mile mark according to the GPS system. At the same time we were getting a bit tense. We were still unsure as to the ease with which we would be able to cross. Suddenly it felt as though someone had punched me in the small of my back. I thought at first that the luggage inside the car had shifted yet again and had fallen forward. We stopped and on inspection found that the rear suspension had sheared completely. The shock absorber had been punched right through the floor pan. There was a gaping hole behind my seat where the leaf spring had been pushed through and we could clearly see the road below. In fact we could touch the road through the floor pan because the car's body, with the suspension shattered, was literally sitting on the road itself. We weren't going to go anywhere for a while. This really was a major disaster. It would be extremely difficult to repair at the best of times and in this remote spot all but impossible, I thought. So near and yet so far.

Just to add to our concerns we saw that the damaged floor was now pushing against the fuel pipe. If that were cut then it would almost certainly mark the end of our whole trip.

Strangely, neither of us expressed any anger or worry. I think we had become so philosophical regarding what fate constantly threw at us that we took it in our stride. The first thing we did was to take out our last bottle of vodka and we sat down at the roadside and, very calmly, thought through what options might be available to us. We certainly couldn't call out the AA – that was for sure!

After a while a small lorry drove past and stopped. Two men jumped out and came across. By this time we were so used to helpful characters that we gave no thought to the fact that we could be robbed. Luckily these men proved to be angels in disguise. For many days now we had been travelling through such remote countryside that we felt anyone who lived here had to be self-sufficient. It was fortunate that we were travelling in an ancient Austin Healey and not a modern vehicle. It was a car that could be repaired by almost any one of the locals, I imagined, because they were used to constantly keeping their vital farm vehicles going in order to maintain their livelihoods. Sure enough, after spending a couple of hours jacking up our car and wedging a temporary heavy metal plate between the floor pan and the remains of the suspension, the car was clear of the ground again and could be moved, albeit very carefully, on its own wheels. We were summoned to drive slowly and follow them. We did as we were told. We took a small side road through the forest and in a couple of miles found ourselves in a village. Needless to say we were the centre of attraction and everyone in the village came out to have a look at us.

We drove to a small wooden house (they were *all* small wooden houses) and were pushed into the front yard. We were asked to go inside and were introduced to the family. Many in that village were related to one another. We met the grandparents, the son who had taken charge of us, his beautiful wife, their two young daughters and sundry brothers, sisters and cousins. The car was forgotten for a while as we were bidden to go and clean ourselves up and join the family for a meal.

The son, Alexei, took us across the road to the grandfather's house and then into a shed in the back garden. We were asked to take our clothes off. This was the one and only time that I became a little cautious, not knowing quite what was likely to happen next! I need have had no concerns. The grandfather had built his own sauna. We were showered in hot water, then in cold and then in hot again. It felt absolutely marvellous. I dare not think how long it had been since I had last had a thorough clean. I felt unbelievably refreshed after that.

We were taken back to the house for a meal and the family had pulled out all the stops for their honoured guests. All the produce, I later discovered, had come from the garden, with the one exception of a bottle of Russian champagne which they had been saving for a special occasion. We had delicious duck meat cooked to perfection from the ducks they kept in the backyard. We had a wide range of salads, hot vegetables, breads and a variety of sweet dishes to follow. We hadn't seen food like this for some time. It was all the more delicious for being so totally unexpected.

The little house had but one bedroom but this was cleared for our use. I do think that some people in the West (me for one!) have a lot to learn from these poor Siberian peasants in the art of simple human kindness. I was sorry that we were not going to reach China that night but our spell in that Siberian house proved to one of the most interesting 'excursions' possible. It gave me the best insight yet into the life of a typical Siberian local.

By this time we had picked up perhaps a couple of dozen phrases in Russian. For very short conversations centred on specific subjects that was fine. It was a different matter conversing over a much longer period. However, with the usual combination of sign language and use of dictionaries, we were able to communicate reasonably well. The strangest thing was their little daughter, who must have been about eight years old. She used to come up to us and babble away in Russian for several minutes. Naturally we had no idea what she was saying. We then nodded and said 'yes' in English and she went away again very happy. This happened time and time again and I don't think she had a clue that we never understood a word. She was a very pretty little girl with a beautiful smile and we took to her straight away.

After dinner we went out and worked on the car until about midnight.

In the morning we were given a full breakfast, consisting of pancakes, cream, eggs, tomatoes, toast, tea and fresh juice. Despite external appearances they certainly ate well in this part of the world. I hadn't really eaten any sweet things whilst in Russia so I was particularly taken with the honey that they produced from hives in the back of their garden. It was, quite literally, like nectar.

The grandfather showed us a collection of stones that he had gathered from the area over the years. It did illustrate what a variety of gems, fossils and rocks could be found. I had no idea if any serious geological work had ever been carried out in this area but I suspected that it would yield a few surprises if the variety that we were shown was anything to go by.

I was beginning to get a little concerned that even if the Chinese had received a communication from Victoria with a new ETA, we were already running two days late. There was a reasonable chance that they had heard nothing since we last managed to make contact from Novosibirsk. In that case we were already over four days overdue. I had no idea how these things worked but I just hoped they would somehow keep somebody 'on duty' at the border to await our eventual arrival. There was no chance of making contact from this unnamed village as there weren't even any telephone lines. It had been even longer since I had spoken to Jenny at home so I trusted that she continued to believe in the old maxim 'no news is good news'.

Unbeknown to me, at the very time that these thoughts had been crossing my mind, Jenny, sitting at her breakfast table nearly 6,000 miles away, had just received a shock. I had found it increasingly difficult to contact home since leaving Moscow. Some of the contacts who met us as we reached the various city limits worked directly for Cadbury's or for one of their agents, particularly those contacts we met in the early stages of our Siberian crossing. They had access to fax contact with Cadbury's in Moscow. One of my jobs was to write an account of our daily experiences so that every two or three days, say, we would be able to give it to our new-found friends, who would in turn relay it back to Moscow. Moscow would then forward it to Chris

Capstick in Bournville, Birmingham. The idea was that he would then distribute the news to a range of individuals, including our own wives, and to a number of local newspapers and radio stations. At least that was the theory and it worked well to begin with but began to break down a bit the further east we went.

Our last communication had included details of our incident with the gun on entering Novosibirsk. For some reason Chris had not spoken directly to Jenny for some time but our local newspaper, the *Herts and Essex Observer*, regularly featured our news whenever they received fresh information, which they duly did for this incident. Given a bit of journalistic licence, they had put this as front-page news, with the headline 'Local man held at gunpoint'. So Jenny, having heard nothing from us for over two weeks, suddenly read for the first time a second-hand (or third- or fourth-hand!) account, over breakfast, in the presence of my younger children, of her husband's seemingly dangerous escapades. She was startled, to say the least, but had the presence of mind to remain calm in front of the children. When they had left for school she made several frantic phone calls to try and find out the sequel.

The car was finished to our satisfaction by midday. The whole village had turned out to lend a hand. Alexei had done an excellent welding job. His tools had been pretty ancient and there appeared no deference to the safety factor. In order to get electricity to power the welding arc, a cable had to be run from a house across the street. There were several flashes of sparking electricity emerging from a variety of places along the cable where the covering had worn away as the process continued. Nobody seemed to care and the children continued to play their ball games, running over this cable from time to time! But who was I to be concerned – they had all survived very well so far without my help!

People here had very little in the material sense but they had good food and shelter and seemed to be some of the happiest and carefree people that I had ever met. We were given a wonderful send-off from the whole village as we left in the early afternoon, having been given yet another delicious meal just before departure. We tried to give them money for their time, hospitality and work but they would accept nothing. When we tried to give some dollars 'for the future of the children' they still refused. The best we could force them to accept were a few souvenirs: our remaining cassette tapes and a couple of T-shirts. What wonderful people! The last two days had been, for me, a most marvellous experience. Given our earlier deep concerns on discovery of the suspension failure, we seemed to prove the maxim that every cloud had a silver lining.

We were so close to the border that we expected to make it in two hours. We believed that the car now had a good inch of extra clearance which seemed to make all the difference. We wondered if, despite our regular inspections, the suspension had been slowly collapsing for some time and this had gradually and persistently been reducing clearance. This would not have been noticeable on a day-to-day basis but perhaps had been the real cause of our very frequent exhaust problems over the last couple of weeks.

The final 25-mile stretch of road turned out to be the worst ever and we averaged 7 m.p.h. Instead of two hours it took us nearly four, which meant that we reached the border town of Zabaykalsk at 6 p.m. Nevertheless we still expected to be in China later that evening. Little did we ·know the considerable problems that still lay ahead.

6

The Sino-Soviet Border

Despite the fact that this really was a one-street town, we just couldn't find the border! This was ridiculous. We asked a passer-by, who pointed out a very small dirt track that ran towards a railway yard. We couldn't believe it. We took this tiny turning and drove past a few railway sidings. There were no signposts at all and we were simply following one of the tracks between two railway lines. We turned a couple of corners and came up against a swing barrier, which was indeed the start of the Sino-Soviet border crossing. We could see a yard behind this which was somewhat reminiscent to me of the East-West Berlin border posts such as the famous Checkpoint Charlie in the Soviet days. There were a couple of pits over which vehicles had to stop as they were searched. Beyond these pits, about 100 yards further on, there was a very large pair of solid metal gates, which was the start of no man's land.

There was no other traffic about, at least not any that was crossing the border. There were quite a few people milling around, however. I jumped out of the car and gave our passports and Russian visa papers to one of the armed guards. He looked at them quizzically. He took them across to an enormous building and returned about ten minutes later. He was accompanied by several soldiers including one with huge colourful epaulettes who turned out to be the border commander.

'Good afternoon,' I said. 'I trust our papers are all in order. We are English,' I added somewhat unnecessarily.

'No, they are not in order,' he replied. 'This is not an international border crossing. It is impossible to cross here

132

unless you are a Chinese or Russian diplomat. It is entirely out of the question. You will have to go back to Moscow.'

I couldn't believe it. Nobody had warned us of this problem. Why hadn't the Russian embassy, when granting us our visa, pointed out that our proposed exit point was not an international crossing? Nawal tried to engage the commander in conversation in order to explain things but he refused to listen and marched back to the barracks. We tried to follow him but were immediately stopped, at gun-point, by the armed guard.

What could we do? It was impossible to go back to Moscow, 4,500 miles behind us. We were exhausted, had no money, had run out of time and, anyway, the car was in no fit state to repeat the journey of the last few weeks. Yet it was equally impossible to go forward faced with armed guards and the huge border gates. The third and final option, to stay in Zabaykalsk and try to sort it out, also appeared impossible as we had only $40 left to our name. My nightmare scenario that I had given a little thought to on several previous occasions during the trip without ever being able to come up with any answer was actually upon us. We could just see the tip of a hill about half a mile away which we knew was China. Again – so near and yet so far! Coming after several days of elation this was the lowest point of the trip. I felt shattered. What on earth could we possibly do?

Nawal tended to come into his own on these occasions. He didn't get mad, which was a good start. He took a shrewd decision that proved absolutely correct. Despite repeated efforts by the armed guard to get us to move our car back to the village, we simply refused to budge. We were not actually blocking anyone's way, yet we were visible to everyone around. That was just the point. If we disap-peared then we would no longer be a problem to the guards and they would forget about us. The longer we stayed there, then the more of an issue we would become and the more they would have to be drawn in to finding a solution. It was good logic and it worked.

While we waited we saw just one vehicle – a small van with four Chinese – about to cross the border. Nawal rushed across and hastily scribbled a note explaining our predicament. He asked if there was any chance that the driver would give it to someone called Jerry Li who should be waiting for us at the Chinese border post. It was a bit of a long shot to say the least. Still, they seemed happy enough to give it a try.

After some considerable time two young ladies came towards us from the barracks and one said, in perfect English, 'We can see your car from our office, where we work as interpreters. I am aware of your problem. If you wait here for a while we are expecting the local trade minister to come by. Perhaps he is in a position to help you.' We went on to have a very friendly chat about matters in general and they then left us for their homes in the village. Sure enough, about an hour later we were approached by a small young man who introduced himself as Valery. He had a small clutch of officials with him. It was apparent that even in this short time the whole village was talking about the two foreigners with the strange car at the border post. Valery explained that he was the director of Sino Co, which, apparently, is a Russian government body responsible for relations and for trade between China and Russia. Valery's oft-repeated phrase was that he was 'a mini foreign office'. He asked us to come with him and he took us to the local police station, where we parked the car.

We were then taken to his office, where, once we had been given a cup of tea ('*chai bes sacre*' was always our rejoinder – tea without sugar please) we sat down. He said that he was due to hold a summit meeting with his opposite number in China in two days' time. He proposed to put our problem on the agenda. On hearing this I had visions of our situation developing into some sort of international incident. As we were in his hands and he seemed to have taken at least some responsibility for us, we didn't argue. Besides, we couldn't think of any alternative. Our more immediate problem was that we had nowhere to stay for the night. He explained that he was sorry but he couldn't possibly put us up for the night because he lived in a very tiny two-roomed flat and there just wasn't enough room for us as well. Again Nawal came to the fore, on the same logic that the more of a problem we were for him the more obliged he would feel to find a solution. Nawal more or less insisted that we had no alternative other than to spend the night with him. I was rather impressed with Nawal because here he was pitting his not inconsiderable negotiating skills with a professional diplomat. Nawal won hands down and we found we had been offered floor space for the night. 'But just for the one night, I'm afraid,' said Valery. I remember thinking, I wouldn't bet on it, Valery, if I were you.

It was suggested that we could take the car to the private lock-up garage of the local police chief. If it wasn't safe there then it wouldn't be safe anywhere, I thought. By this time it was getting late so we went back to Valery's flat, which was indeed tiny, and bedded down in our sleeping bags on the wooden floor amidst the stink and fumes of thick cigarette smoke.

In the morning, after a breakfast of bread, pickled herrings and vodka (!), Valery said that he would leave us for a while but perhaps we would like to call on him at his office later in the morning. The town was small and everywhere was within walking distance. It was a very scruffy town and this added to my general air of depression. We walked to the international telephone exchange at the other end of the street and tried to put a call through to Ma Dan in Beijing but failed to get through to her, or to anyone else. We sat on the top of a small hill and looked across a valley and past all the rolls of barbed wire and other security devices. We saw the hills of northern China and had such a good view that we could even make out the buildings in the nearest town, the Chinese border post of Manzhouli, 6 miles away. But it could have been a million miles for all the difficulties that we now faced.

I refused to contemplate the possibility of driving all the way back again. Surely this would be impossible. But try as we might, it was difficult to think of how we could get out of this one. Our mood wasn't helped by the fact that we really weren't sure if anybody in the outside world knew where we were. Deep down, logic told me that we just needed to communicate with the right people and all would be well. We would get through. But how did we get the key to finding the right people? There was another meeting to be held later that day between senior border guards from both sides in an attempt to improve relationships and communication channels between the two countries. Valery had asked us to see him again before this meeting just in case there was something else in our story that he wasn't aware of that might help unlock the problem. I must say that I had long since considered that we might have difficulty getting into China but I had never considered that we would have a problem getting out of Russia. Was it a question of giving a bribe to the local commander? If so, how much did we give? Where did we get the money? Would this just land us in deeper trouble? Why didn't any of the Russian embassy officials in London or any of the other officials en route point out to us that this wasn't a regular border crossing? After all, we had made our exact route known when we applied for the visa in the first place and they had actually stamped it on our Russian visa. And anyway, what was the problem in letting us out? Why should the Russians care about us *leaving* their country? What problem would it cause them? Surely if there was a problem then it would be with the Chinese immigration people not the Russians. Even if they thought we were the most desperate rogues in the world, it would have been in their interests to let us out, surely. With these and many other thoughts crossing my mind, we decided to stroll back to Valery's office and see if there were any new developments.

Valery greeted me kindly enough and said that there was an important job he would like me to do. Great, I thought, this is the start of getting the correct papers together to allow us out.

136

'I would like you to listen to this tape recording of a Paul McCartney song and write down all the words in English for me please,' said Valery. 'It is one of my favourite songs but I have never fully understood the meaning behind it,' he explained in passable but stilted English. What a strange country, I thought. It didn't help that I spent the next half-hour writing down little more than 'Do dee do, coo coo chi coo'. I took the decision that I wouldn't try to explain this to Valery, I'd just tell him I had written it all down and had left a note for him to read later. What a ridiculous situation to be in. However, we needed as much help as we could get, so we needed to keep Valery on our side. Nothing much happened at all and we spent hour after hour waiting in a dull room in Valery's office complex. I wondered how many days would be spent like this before something, anything, happened to break the monotony. I tried to stop myself getting depressed again.

Suddenly Valery appeared and introduced two Chinese-looking gentlemen from a company called Sinotrans. They handed me a note which read as follows:

BEIJING GOLDEN FRIEND INTERNATIONAL TRAVEL SERVICE

Dear Nawal and David

I'm Julian King your interpreter from Beijing Golden Friend International Travel Service. I'm glad to hear that you've arrived at the border. First of all, on behalf of Ms Ma Dan from Cadbury I warmly welcome you to China.

Maybe you have some difficulties in passing the Sino-Russian border. But take it easy, I asked Mr Li from Sinotrans Co. Manzhouli branch to help you deal with the problems.

By the way Mr Zhou Guangyu from Cadbury Beijing office is also waiting for you in Manzhouli.

Trust me and everything will be fine!

Mr Li will help you contact us by phone today. Also,

Mr Jeff and Ms Ma Dan will wait your phone call all day today.

Best regards

Julian King

I suffered yet another mood swing. Or should I say enjoyed one, because this was in the right direction. One minute I was fighting off depression and the next I was finding it difficult to curb my joy and excitement. Surely this meant that we were going to make it after all. There couldn't be any problems after this. Or could there? At least we were now sure that the outside world knew where we were. Not only that but there was optimism, even confidence, expressed in the note that all would be well. We had also been introduced to professionals who, presumably, were well versed in the art of overcoming Russian obstinacy.

I was intrigued to know how Julian King had got to know of our plight. There were two possibilities. Firstly that the note we had 'smuggled' across the previous day had got through. The second, and in my view the most likely, was that Valery had made contact with his opposite number in China: Julia (strange name for a Chinaman, I thought!). He (or she?) had contacted Ma Dan, who had pulled a few strings with the border guards via the agents that she had been using and to whom a great deal of our money had been paid over.

It was afternoon by this stage and, after thanking Valery profusely, we were taken by our new-found Chinese friends to a small but extremely comfortable hotel adjacent to the border crossing. Sinotrans, apparently, owned the hotel. They were by far the most active agents for effecting crossings of people and goods between the two countries and had been in operation since the end of the Second World War. They told us that they had never heard of anybody other than Russian or Chinese traders or officials crossing the border at this particular point. Not only would we be the first Englishmen or the first Europeans but also the first foreigners of any nationality to get across, they said. This added to our sense of achievement. But we weren't quite there yet! We had no idea what had been going on behind the scenes but we were assured that all the paperwork was now in order. All that was required now, apparently, was for the regional Russian commander, based back in Chita, to give his formal approval. 'How long would that take?' we asked. There was a shrug in reply. We were taken down and given an excellent meal in the hotel restaurant (for free!).

After the meal we went up to the office again. A message came through that the final permissions had been granted and we had been given a crossing slot of 4 p.m. that afternoon. Given that we were the only vehicle to cross that day and, as far as I know, possibly the only one for the week, I was intrigued to know why we were being treated as though we were an aeroplane trying to fly through congested air space. 'That's the way things are in Russia,' I was told. It was some evidence of the brainwashed state of my mind by this stage that I accepted that as a full and reasonable answer!

We felt like potential escapees from a prisoner of war camp. We were huddled together in this little room with numerous Chinese people just waiting for all the conditions to come together simultaneously before we 'made a break for it'.

At 3.30 p.m., just half an hour before the Big Moment, we were taken to the home of the police chief to retrieve our car in readiness to make our slot time. He was out and the garage was locked! No amount of prising at the doors could release them and nobody knew exactly where he was. All of a sudden half a dozen Chinese helpers appeared and, each with a mobile phone (essential kit in this part of the world), they made numerous phone calls. We could only guess what was happening and I assume an 'all stations alert' call was going out to local policemen to find their chief. Half an hour later he was found in a neighbouring village visiting his relatives. He was driven back at speed and unlocked his garage door. However, we had now missed our slot. Knowing how things work in Russia, this could mean a significant delay despite the illogicality of it all. We went back to the office and more phone calls were made. We were given a new slot of 6 p.m. just 20 minutes away. We rushed to pack and were escorted front and rear by large overland vehicles flying Russian and Chinese flags on their roofs.

We were taken down the little mud track that we had discovered earlier, to the accompaniment of shouts and cheers from the villagers. We reached the border post and the very same commander came out to see us. There was no mention of the earlier problems; it was as though he had just met us for the first time. Presumably, in the interim, someone had given him his cut of the fee, I thought. Several soldiers came up as we parked over the pit to have a look at what was going on. It was smiles all round. Our Sinotrans officials disappeared into the office to complete the mountain of paperwork that was necessary. Having experienced the paperwork required when ordering a boiled egg for breakfast at a Russian hotel, I dreaded to think what was required for a first ever crossing of an international border. And this was a border which had been fought over many times in the past. A border between two nuclear powers. A border that no European had crossed before. It really was a big moment for us. We chatted away patiently and, eventually, the officials reappeared smiling. We were off!

Still with an escort front and rear, we set off from the Russian compound and through the large metal gates at the end. About 50 yards further on we passed under a large bridge with the letters *CCCP* emblazoned upon it. We entered a stretch of no man's land. Another 100 yards and we passed under a similar bridge but this time with Chinese characters inscribed upon it. *We were in China.*

We passed through a heavily armed metal gate a little further on and were stopped by a squad of soldiers. What could go wrong now? I thought. There was no need for concern. These small men in pristine uniforms were all smiles. They insisted on having their photographs taken at the side of the car one at a time. This took several minutes but it didn't matter. Eventually we were waved on and entered a compound. There were perhaps a hundred people milling around and a series of small offices arranged around the perimeter. In the middle of the crowd there were about a dozen people wearing blue Cadbury's shirts. One came forward and introduced himself as Jerry Zhou and a second as Julian King 'but everyone calls me JinBo'.

'Welcome to China,' he said. Those words were music to my ears! I literally cried with joy and emotion.

I don't know to what extent the crowd had been organised by them or whether there was always a number of people hanging around. There didn't appear to be any other traffic coming across the border. There were many press photographers there and we were asked to pose for the cameras. Our car stickers were changed. The Russian Cadbury slogans were peeled off and new brightly coloured posters in Chinese script were attached to the side of each door. JinBo, the interpreter, who became known to us as 'the Red Army spy', became a very good friend. Considering that the People's Liberation Army had, quite literally, formally approved him, he was very different to my expectations. He spoke excellent English, albeit with a heavy American accent, he was young (early twenties), he was full of fun and his big claim to fame was that he had climbed Mount Everest the previous year. From that moment he took charge of us and this lasted all the way to Beijing, where he, reluctantly, handed us over to Jeff Briggs, the Australian boss of Cadbury's China. But that was later in the story. For the moment, he asked us to go into one of the nearby offices and we started to fill in forms. There was a considerable amount of paperwork but, with JinBo's help, we got through it in about an hour. We were then taken the remaining few miles into Manzhouli, where we were shown to our rooms in a very pleasant hotel.

Just about everything in China differed from my expectations. For a start the short road into town from the border itself was tarmac surfaced. This was a forgotten luxury. The car just glided across, not knowing why it had suddenly deserved this treat. We couldn't believe the relative silence. No regular thumps and bangs as we bounced off one boulder and on to the next! The car really had done us proud. Although we had stopped for repairs on too many occasions, a less robust car would have given up the ghost long ago. This was a tough one and we had needed it to be.

Russia had been a great deal more basic in terms of overall living standards and quality of hotels than I had imagined. There, people lived very tough lives, eking out an existence from the soil in very harsh conditions.

In China we would see many first-class hotels, a wide variety of restaurants and, in the cities, department stores which stocked the very latest in quality goods such as computers and video-recording machines. And all this was observed in cities where very few Europeans had visited. This was not Beijing, where the expat and tourist communities were so large that they could have, by themselves no doubt, supported several luxury stores. That is not to say that a great many Chinese don't lived in poverty, I am sure they do. All I can say is that we saw a large number of Chinese people living better-quality lives than those who had the misfortune to be born on the other side of the border in Russia. China held many more surprises for me, as I discovered later in our stay.

We stayed for three days in Manzhouli. Much of this time was spent being ushered from one government building to another in order to complete all the necessary documentation for our entry. I had always thought that the Russians delighted in bureaucracy and had elevated it to an art form, but I hadn't by then had experience of the Chinese playing the same game. I now believe that the Chinese are the world champions. The procedure included being issued with Chinese licence plates for the car. I was told that in order to obtain the visa, the Cadbury officials had to obtain the permission of no less than 23 government departments. It was the People's Liberation Army who had proved the most difficult and they were the ones who had insisted on us being accompanied at all times by an approved official. As it turned out, we were delighted with this decision because JinBo proved a major asset for us on many occasions. Yet again, as with many other incidents on our journey, what we had originally considered a major concern turned into a positive benefit. I was so grateful that fate continued to deal us good hands!

Manzhouli itself was very much smarter than any of the Siberian towns that we had encountered. The streets were well maintained and clean. There were many shops, all with attractive items for sale, and they were similar to the sort of shops one might come across in any Western European town.

The hotel where we were located was also owned by the Sinotrans company. It was actually run by a Mr Li, who proved to be a very affable fellow. We had been used to being on our own in the evenings but in Manzhouli, and indeed for the rest of our trip, we usually had an entourage of several people. The three dinners that we enjoyed during our stay in this hotel were splendid affairs. There were usually at least a dozen of us at each sitting. The food was varied and plentiful. It was washed down with very passable Chinese wine. At the end of the meal there were the invariable toasts. Everyone was expected to make a little speech (which was then repeated by the translator – JinBo – into the other language). There were hearty roars of approval as the compliments flowed from one side to the other in a most extreme manner. For example we were welcomed as 'the intrepid explorers from the ancient Kingdom of England. We are delighted to have the eternal pleasure of being the first to welcome such illustrious travellers to our humble province. It is a deeply felt honour that we will treasure in our hearts for ever. . .' etc. etc. It was, of course, way over the top but nobody cared and it was an excuse to drink a toast after each speech. We managed to knock back a couple of dozen small phials of very sweet, but very potent, Chinese liqueur in this fashion each evening.

We were able to contact our families and this was the first time I had spoken to Jenny for over two weeks. It was great to be able to tell her that the trip had already proved a success and that we had achieved our main objective as we were now in China. She then told me about her earlier concerns after having read the local newspaper headlines about our escapades in Novosibirsk. I realised just how much she had worried and how difficult it had been for her, not just regarding this particular incident, but for the whole of the trip. We had never been apart for so long before. She had been so supportive throughout and had been correct in her original advice that the prospects this trip offered would be too good for me to miss. I had enjoyed a most amazing time and I was the one having fun while she had had to continue alone with all the repetitive routine that makes up a large part of active family life. I really missed her a lot at that moment.

We discussed and agreed our itinerary with the Cadbury team. They wanted us to visit several of the northern cities where they had opened stores and had organised a small presentation or function in each of these in order to gain maximum publicity.

We were also introduced to the PR team, which, again, was comprised of some great characters. They tended to drive ahead in a couple of vans and we met up every third day or so whenever a press conference or other function had been arranged.

During our stay in Manzhouli I had a lengthy conversation with several people regarding life in China and the political system. I had been brought up to believe that there was terrible abuse of human rights in China. I realise that the country is huge and we were only seeing a tiny part of it. Furthermore I have no doubt that the system in China is very much harsher in certain ways than that that we are used to in the UK. I am sure many are persecuted simply for their political beliefs and I am also aware of the history of the poor Tibetan people in recent decades. However, on this trip I can only repeat my direct experiences and the truth was that everyone we met, including many impromptu encounters with people we simply happened to bump in to, seemed pretty happy and content with their lot.

Mr Li, the manager of the hotel, one evening brought up the subject of the 'one child per family' policy. Everyone round the table agreed that this policy was absolutely necessary, given the population growth of the country. There were 1.2 billion Chinese according to the last official census, but most there believed that the true figure was perhaps as much as 50 per cent higher than this. The 'one child per family' policy was vital to curb further growth and everyone was supportive. On an associated matter, I had assumed that China's attitude towards its minorities was appalling. I was surprised to hear that the government appeared to be doing all they could to ensure the continuity of the minority ethnic groups in the country. For example, Mr Li came from a different ethnic 'tribe' and he was, therefore, exempt from the 'one child' policy. As proof, he introduced us to his three daughters, two of whom worked for the hotel.

The food in China proved to be very good. There was little in the way of sweet items. Even for breakfast we were eating braised vegetables, soup, savoury dumplings, rice and meats. There were no jams, marmalades, cornflakes, pancakes or sugar to be found anywhere. Given my erstwhile middle-age spread, this was a good thing. I weighed myself on our first night in Manzhouli and discovered I had lost 1½ stones during our four weeks in Siberia. I was looking rather better for it as well.

We made a list of the many items that were going to be freighted on to Beijing to await our arrival, as we made room for JinBo in the back of the car. By that stage of the journey it was quite easy to dump a large percentage of our baggage. We no longer needed any of the Polish and Russian maps or guide books. We also had no further requirement for the jerrycans or oil cans that had taken up so much room. Needless to say, we had already jettisoned our planks in Zabaykalsk! We also pared down even further on the clothes we would take with us.

I managed to get quite a bit of exercise in the form of long walks around the town. Although I had managed to keep my weight down, this was achieved by eating very little and by spending most of the day in a mobile sauna. After several weeks largely spent inside the tiny Healey cockpit it was nice to spend a couple of days enjoying the fresh air and taking a stroll.

We sent a number of faxes to our normal list of contacts: Chris Capstick at Cadbury's in the UK, the office of the Children in Crisis charity, Reuters, and an onward fax to the awaiting team in Beijing. We also talked a lot to the Chinese press, who were interested in our story. There was often quite a political bias to their questions, which was interesting. For example, we were frequently asked variations on the following theme: 'Gentlemen, we are very grateful that you have shown an interest in our country and have come to visit us. We welcome you. However, we understand that you have been raising funds to assist in the building of an orphanage. What makes you think that we, the Chinese people, cannot provide adequate facilities ourselves for our orphans?' Actually it was a perfectly reasonable question but we just had to be careful how we answered it to avoid giving unnecessary offence.

Friday, 28 June was our last day in the border town of Manzhouli. We had breakfast that morning with Jerry Zhou and enjoyed the usual vast array of different dishes as we ate in a private room set aside for us.

I went out to look over the car. I noted the mileage reading and calculated that we had travelled 6,420 miles from home so far. We were actually now used to talking in terms of kilometres as this was what everyone in China and Russia understood. I did a quick calculation to express this in kilometres to Jerry. We estimated that it would take us 10 days to reach Beijing and then we wanted to spend a few days there before flying home. No doubt Cadbury's would want us to do some PR work for them in the capital and we also had other matters to arrange such as the shipment of the car back home. However, we were also very keen to do a little bit of sightseeing, so our exact stay in Beijing, like everything else on the trip, was likely to be changeable depending on circumstances at the time. I had mixed views about staying on in China too long. I was very keen to see as much of it as I could, but, on the other hand, I would have been away from home for over seven weeks, which was long enough.

Jerry then took our various bits of surplus baggage with him. JinBo had left at 5 a.m. to get the final permission from the local police headquarters for our onward travel. The idea was that he would be back in the early afternoon. We would have lunch together and the three of us would then depart for our next destination, Yakeshi, which I calculated should be only about four hours away. We got a message that there was a last-minute problem with our authorisations and JinBo, who was at the neighbouring town of Hailar, was trying to sort it out. We started lunch without him but, luckily, he appeared half-way through with a broad smile on his face and brandishing our newly made-up Chinese number plates. He was also brandishing our passports and I saw that mine now sported a rather attractive-looking hand stamp which was my entry visa to China. Because I was a car driver and was entering at Manzhouli I saw that it was numbered 0001!

These final clearances meant that all the last-minute hurdles had been overcome. We enjoyed the rest of the meal and, after a short but well-attended farewell ceremony in the hotel foyer, various vehicles escorted us to the city limit. More farewells were made there and then we were off. The road was good, our spirits were high and, the biggest luxury of the lot, the road surface, at least at this stage, was excellent. I was very excited that officialdom was behind us and the adventure of China itself, commencing with the northern regions of Inner Mongolia, lay just ahead.

147

7

China

We had stayed in Manzhouli for three days – purely to satisfy the documentation requirements of the various government agencies, although I for one was thankful for the three days' enforced relaxation. Considering that these formalities were being concluded on our behalf by a team of experienced Chinese officials and they still took three days, it was clear that we would have stood no chance at all had we tried to get through on our own. Manzhouli had been an active town. On two occasions during our three-day stay we had seen a convoy of lorries from Russia stocking up with vast quantities of every conceivable consumer item. In Zabaykalsk we had never seen the Chinese purchasing items from the Russians. It was a surprise to me that trade appeared to be just the one way, and this again challenged my indoctrinated view of China being a poor country in desperate need of just about everything. Here they were organising a very active, and no doubt profitable, export business with the 'have-nots' from the other side of the border.

The other noticeable feature was that massive Russian women invariably drove the lorries. If they had had the sort of suspension problems that we had suffered, they looked as though they would simply pick up the vehicle and walk away with it!

As we left the Manzhouli environs we saw very little in the way of habitation. It was very barren countryside. This was the China that I had expected. In this northern part of Inner Mongolia the road wound lazily around hillsides with breathtaking views of waterfalls and valleys.

We began to get to know JinBo and he taught us a few Chinese phrases. He would ensure that we got the pronunciation just right before he would let us move on to the next one. He was a good teacher. We even sang a few Chinese songs! The atmosphere was very good. We felt that we had already overcome the biggest test of the trip, namely the 4,500 challenging miles from Moscow. We also knew that if we had any problems from here on then at least we could call on some friendly faces who would be able to get us some help. It was a very reassuring feeling and so different to our worries when in Siberia. However, all was not plain sailing, as the next few days would tell.

In the middle of nowhere we passed three horsemen in full Mongolian costumes and we slowed down to take photographs. They were just as interested in us as we were in them. We had a chat, made so much easier, of course, by having our own in-house interpreter. I had forgotten how quickly one could get a point across when talking to locals if speaking the same language! The tribesmen invited us back to their tent for tea. This was an opportunity not to be missed. A little further on, just off the road, we came across about half a dozen tents. They were somewhat similar to Red Indian teepees but were more rounded in shape at the top. Here we were invited in and introduced to the rest of the family. We had found that throughout Russia, and later in China, there was a great deal of emphasis on the importance of the family unit. Everyone seemed to pitch in when it came to looking after the children and everyone seemed to take their responsibilities seriously as far as the elderly were concerned. There seemed to be the utmost respect held and shown by the younger generation for the older.

We were given pots of sweet tea. We discussed the contrast between their lifestyle and that enjoyed by the typical Englishman. There was such a huge gulf between the two that we confined our remarks to just one or two key points. The Mongolians scratched a living from the soil by growing certain crops and by rearing cattle and other animals. In summer they supplemented this income by offering their tents as hostelries and provided tea and basic food to passing travellers. Once the summer season was over and travelling became a lot more difficult because of the snow, they would move away from the roadside areas and back to easier grazing land.

After this very pleasant and unusual interlude we resumed our journey to Yakeshi, arriving there at the civilised hour of 8 p.m. When we had arrived at an hotel in Russia, invariably we would have been so late that all facilities for obtaining food would have long since closed. Here we had time for a short stroll to get our bearings and stretch our legs. JinBo showed us a cemetery for Russian soldiers. I was fascinated to see that it was covered in Russian inscriptions which translated as giving thanks to our true Russian friends for helping us repel the invading Japanese. Apparently there were several similar Russian cemeteries in this northern part of China – so I learnt that they hadn't always been antagonistic towards each other.

We soon returned to the hotel and it really was a treat still to have time for a hot shower followed by a very pleasant dinner. Even then we managed to get to bed before the small hours. Life seemed pretty good again!

I woke very early and dozed on and off until 6 a.m. but felt well rested. The hot water in several of the Russian hotels, and in the two so far in China, was only available at certain times. In the case of this hotel in Yakeshi, the Lunchung, it was for one hour in the morning and the same again in the evening. It didn't really worry us, providing we knew when it was. But I never quite understood why. I could understand water not being available at all if there was a supply problem but I couldn't quite work out why the boiler should only work intermittently. I thought China was self-sufficient in hydroelectric power, but perhaps I was wrong.

Our next journey to the city of Qiqihar (pronounced Chi Chi Ha, with the last 'Ha' being loudly stressed – according to JinBo) was supposed to be the one and only leg where there were some bad patches of road. (Now where had I heard that before?) So I was a little apprehensive, having trusted that we had left those problems behind. I just hoped that we wouldn't do any further damage to the car. I'd have hated to have wasted more precious time whilst the exhaust or suspension was being repaired. However, I still felt pretty confident, having survived the Siberian experiences. Surely things couldn't be as bad as that, I thought. Sadly, this confidence was later to prove misplaced!

We breakfasted at 7 a.m. and were expecting to be away very shortly afterwards. There was much less to do now that we didn't have the daily ritual of having to pack everything back into (and on) the car. This had been quite an art, given the amount of baggage that we were carrying in the small space available. It was rather like piecing together a giant jigsaw puzzle where every item had its own particular place and fitted exactly. Now we only had one small rucksack of personal effects each, plus cameras and a small bag for me containing some maps, pens and a few other navigational aids. That was it.

We did indeed set off on schedule but by midday we were very frustrated with our slow rate of progress. The rough surface had been bad enough to necessitate a very slow crawl for the last 100 miles and every time we asked the occasional bystander, the reply constantly appeared to be that it was 'just another 30 kilometres [20 miles] and then the road surface would improve'.

Nawal insisted that we pull in to the grounds of a small office at the side of the road which appeared to be the headquarters of the road repair team and ask them for some tea. I doubted whether we would get much of a response but I was wrong. They responded as though they were a fully-fledged café: tea all round plus biscuits. They were keen to know what on earth we were doing and, of course, with JinBo around, the explanations were much easier to effect.

By mid-afternoon we were still struggling to come to terms with the road surface and were also getting very hungry. As we passed through a small village JinBo asked

151

us to keep a lookout for two red lanterns. This, apparently, was the sign of a restaurant. 'Every village should have one', he insisted, and sure enough he was proved right. The one and only table in this particular one was taken, so the lady in charge asked us into her bedroom! This was an entirely innocent invitation and she proceeded to set out a makeshift table and asked us what we wanted. I've no idea what JinBo replied but even in a tiny village like this we found that in no time at all about a dozen delicious-looking dishes were placed before us. This was in great contrast to our experiences in Russia. All the dishes were explained to us by the lady of the house in Chinese, which JinBo translated for us. There were the usual ones of prawns and of chicken and special fried rice. But we laughed at the last two described as 'especially strong fungus' and 'unidentified animal meat'! Despite their unusual descriptions I have to say that all the dishes tasted delicious.

After our late lunch we resumed our battle with the road but by 10 p.m. we were still a long way from home. The poor road surface had lasted 200 miles. I stress again that 'bad' in this context does not simply mean that there was the odd puddle or bump but that the whole surface was littered with loose stones, some measuring several inches in height and width, together with severe ruts sometimes a couple of feet deep. This might be acceptable for a lorry with a wheelbase height of several feet, but our lowly 4 inches caused the usual problems and we blew the exhaust pipe twice. On each occasion it took about an hour to patch up with makeshift bandages made from metal sheet. It was still blowing thereafter but appeared to have improved and was good enough, if it held, for us to complete the journey. However, with only 2 miles left before we hit a decent surface again, we hit a problem.

It had been raining very hard for several hours and, in the dark, we could make out a narrow chicane in the road as it passed through a village. There was no way round this short stretch. It was covered in mud, with pools of water lying at the bottom of the two ruts at each side of the road and it was therefore impossible to judge the depth. Right in the middle of this difficult patch we got completely stuck. We could not move in either direction. Within seconds, what had been a deserted scene began to fill up with an audience from the whole village of perhaps 200 people, even though it was the middle of the night and pitch-dark! There were enough helpers to volunteer to wade into the muddy pools to try and pull us out but it soon became clear that manpower alone was not enough to shift us. We were all completely covered in mud at this stage and still it continued to rain. The local farmer was called for and he attached his tractor to the front of the Healey. Even this was not enough to release the suction that the mud had created as it stuck to the underside of the car. A larger tractor was called for and with the two machines in tandem we were eventually pulled out, much to the amusement of all the onlookers. I think we provided the cabaret show for them for that evening and I expect they talked about the incident for a long time thereafter. We were on our way again by 1 a.m. We didn't have too far to go but our troubles were not yet over.

Half an hour later, in the midst of a torrential downpour, we thought we could make out what looked like a wall erected right across the road in front of us. Anyone who has driven a Healey will know that the windscreen wipers fall well short of the efficiencies that modern wipers produce. The screen was covered in smears and we were concentrating hard on bailing out the steady streams of water that were pouring into the car from all sides. We were also very tired so it was difficult to focus on this barrier. As we got closer we made out that the road surface must have been particularly soggy at this spot. The passing of occasional lorries earlier had apparently caused a stretch about 50 yards long where there were just two ruts, one at each side of the road, each about 2 feet deep. The mud had banked up several feet on the outside of these ruts. We stopped and decided that there was no possibility of driving off the road and taking a detour across a field or two in order to meet up with the road a few yards further on. This was a trick that had occasionally come in handy in Russia but that night this particular option was out. The width between the very high external mud banks was wide enough to take the car but there was no room for manoeuvre within. On similar occasions it had sometimes been possible to keep the car on a higher plane by driving to one side, keeping just one of the deep ruts underneath the car and a wheel either side of it. This was not a possibility either. Unfortunately, if we simply drove straight across, our wheels would not touch the ground for most of the distance of about 50 yards. There was no other traffic to help us and the rainfall was increasing the risk of further flooding. We decided that the only chance we had would be to take a run at it. Hopefully if we could get the car straight enough, then the momentum of the machine would ensure that it would slide on its skid shield for several yards until the wheels were able to make contact again. It was quite a risky option but we felt that if the car slewed to one side, it was reasonable to suppose that the high mud banks on either side would at least prevent it from crashing into the deep ditches at either side of the road.

We backed up a bit and said a prayer (in Chinese!). Then, with full revs, we raced towards the mud and soon found ourselves gliding along. Unfortunately we just didn't have enough momentum to make it all the way across and we slowly slid to a halt about 10 yards short. The mud banks on either side were so close that we couldn't open the doors. We had to unscrew the side screens and crawl out of the open windows. We couldn't even get a grip to try and push the car one way or the other. We were absolutely caked in mud. We realised our folly in that the water level was rising rapidly and we were now in such a predicament that another couple of hours or so would see the car totally flooded, which would cause no end of damage. Yet again we were in a situation of our own making where there was no obvious solution.

Fortunately for us, we spied a lorry coming towards us in

the distance. It was lucky that there was a vehicle on the move at all at that time of night and we were luckier still that it was coming from the direction in which we wanted to go. This meant that if we were able to get the lorry to tow us out, then we would end up on the right side of the mud obstacle rather than have to negotiate the problem all over again. The driver was willing to help and had a tow rope in the vehicle. It was a powerful machine so we were hopeful. We were so drenched in water and mud that it made little difference for one of us to scramble around underneath the car. Nawal took big gulps of air from time to time before re-submerging, in order to make a secure fix of the rope on the towing point near the front. Once that procedure had been completed, it took only a few minutes for the car to be dragged out. After giving heartfelt thanks to the driver, who had seemed somewhat bemused by our presence, we were on our way again. We got to our hotel, without further incident, at 5 a.m., just as dawn was breaking! That day had been our worst day so far in terms of time taken and problems encountered. What we had anticipated would be an eight-hour journey had taken twenty-two hours.

We were up reasonably early on the Sunday morning despite the exhausting events of the day before and the very late night. Surprisingly, the previous day had proved one of the best for me. This was because of the team spirit that had been in evidence in the car throughout. Were we becoming seasoned travellers who had seen it all before and were becoming more philosophical as a result, I wondered. The answer was that I didn't know but certainly I had felt calm and relaxed throughout the day and tackled the difficulties in the best fashion I could as and when they had occurred. Between the specific incidents, we had spent plenty of time in the car whilst on the move and had laughed, joked and sung a great deal. It had been good fun. I think another aspect that affected me at this stage was the relief that I continued to feel simply because we had already achieved my first major objective: to get into China. What happened from this point onwards, short of a major disaster, didn't really worry me. China was very different and it was always fascinating when we stopped and talked to the locals. In addition to that, if the truth were known, I found JinBo a breath of fresh air with his relaxed manner and good sense of humour.

We were heading for Harbin on the Sunday and hoped to reach this very large city before dark. I was also getting keen to telephone Jenny as I hadn't spoken to her for over a week and was feeling a bit homesick by now. I could also be fairly sure of finding her in on a Sunday evening. I thought of events at home and remembered that this was the weekend when my eldest son, Daniel, was about to set off for the Caribbean island of Martinique. He had been spending a year of his four-year university language course in France and, through connections there, had landed a two-month summer job at an hotel on this French-speaking island. It would be nice to talk to him before he left.

We left our Qiqihar hotel by mid-morning and, because we had missed breakfast, stopped at a roadside stall to purchase fresh fruit (bananas, apples and pears) to munch along the way. We also filled up with petrol, which was not difficult to find. It cost 50 cents a litre, being more expensive than the Russian average price of 33 cents per litre but still considerably cheaper than in England.

The road was very good, in direct contrast to yesterday's experience. The rain was still in evidence and came down hard but only in short bursts. I took a turn at the wheel myself, the first time I had driven in China. The car still had a tendency to aquaplane with the amount of water around and it was difficult to gauge the depth of the numerous potholes that caused the occasional jolt. We continued to find that, unlike in Russia, roadside cafés were reasonably plentiful and served a variety of good-quality inexpensive food. We were greeted with a studied fascination and often told, via our interpreter, that we were the first foreigners they had ever seen. We became a little blasé at this as it happened so frequently, but it only took a little reflection

156

on this point to be reminded of the highly unusual, indeed unique, nature of our trip.

We passed out of Inner Mongolia and entered what is known locally simply as the north-east region of China. We noticed a lot of hives all along the roadside and eventually stopped to have a closer look. Once again, the locals rushed up to us, this time volunteering to show us inside the hives which they duly did. We first donned protective headgear and then gazed at the millions of bees swarming around inside. There is nothing unusual in this but I made a note of the fact in my diary as yet another incident where the local people took a pride in what they did and were keen to talk and to show us anything about which we expressed curiosity. Far from the inscrutable and reticent characters that I had imagined we would meet throughout China, here again were people only too willing to swap stories and speak quite openly with foreigners.

We later stopped to repair the exhaust, which was blowing a little – perhaps not surprising, given the difficult conditions we had suffered over the last couple of days. It took about an hour to fix – better than average. I wondered just how many times we had repaired the exhaust. I counted this up at the end of the trip, with the assistance of my diary notes, and the total came to exactly 30 times. As usual, on this occasion, a number of assorted vehicles stopped for a chat. One driver advised us of a short cut saving about 12 miles. Would this contain problem stretches of road, we wondered. We decided to give it a go.

We stopped for lunch in the town of Daqing, which was the halfway point on our journey to Harbin. The translation of the town's name, I was told, meant 'Grand Ceremony'. It was founded in 1950 due to the discovery of oil in the region very shortly after 'New China' was formed on 1 October 1949. It was another truly excellent meal with just three dishes to sample this time. We had a mere 120 miles to go and I estimated that we should arrive before 8 p.m. But how many times have my optimistic calculations been shattered, I wondered. In fact the road was excellent all the way and we arrived in the city by 7 p.m. and were outside our hotel by 7.30 p.m.

The Modern Hotel, Harbin, lived up to its name. It really was as good a hotel as I have stayed in anywhere. And it wasn't just a showpiece for Western tourists. It is true that it was here that we met the first Europeans that we had seen since leaving Moscow several weeks before and the first foreigners since meeting the Americans in Novosibirsk. This was a small group of six teachers from Europe and Australia, who were spending a year on an exchange visit for teachers. Chinese nationals, mainly businessmen, occupied the rest of this large hotel. We spent a couple of hours with these teachers in the hotel bar. It was interesting to hear their stories. They were reasonably happy with their lot but the main complaint was that their temporary Chinese bosses paid no heed to their requests to be able to plan ahead. Frequently an edict would come down from the regional education board, changing the dates for holidays, for example, at short notice. This made life difficult for them. Otherwise, they seemed to be enjoying their experience in a very different culture. I retired to my room and luxuriated in a hot bath with plenty of soapsuds. Again, it was amazing just how rewarding and refreshing a little luxury like this was to someone who was unable to enjoy one very frequently. I tried to telephone home. With the time difference it would be just 2 p.m. on Sunday in England, a good time to reach the family. However, it was frustrating to hear my own voice at the other end of the world as my answerphone clicked in.

We went out for a dinner of dumplings (a Chinese speciality) with Jerry Zhou and Eric, who was the local Harbin representative for Cadbury's. I can't say that dumplings were my favourite food. That particular dinner was the least enjoyable of our various meals in China. Nevertheless, it was very good to sample the local delicacies, if only once, assuming one can describe a 'dumpling' as a delicacy!

On the Monday morning we spent a couple of hours tidying up and then cleaning the car. We took the top off and left it in the hotel baggage room. Four of us then spent some time driving around the city of Harbin taking in the sights. The occasional short shower did us no harm at all. In England one of my friends had told me that the Chinese never smile and don't use many facial expressions (hence 'the inscrutable Chinese'). What rubbish! In that city of several millions it seemed half the population had come up to us during our city tour and introduced themselves to us with huge smiles on their faces. They were fascinated with just seeing Europeans, let alone a strange car like ours. I had imagined China to be a country full of poverty, with people frightened to be seen to be talking to foreigners in case 'big brother' was watching. Another fallacy. We were inundated with interested people. We were just driving along the main roads in the city; not following some government-designed route where we would only see the party faithful. I can't imagine that life held the same degree of material comfort for the Chinese as it did for the average Englishman, but life as we saw it in China was at least a lot more acceptable than I had imagined. I never did get used to the sudden cries of 'Whoa' from people who suddenly observed the car, including policemen on traffic duty!

We had an excellent lunch in the Green Fields restaurant and were then taken to a local department store. This was another surprise for me. I was just taken aback with the amount of products available. Very similar to a John Lewis or Debenhams store in the home counties.

In the afternoon Jeff Briggs and Ma Dan, the managing director of Cadbury's in China and his right-hand lady, who happened to have been instrumental in organising this trip for us, flew into town from Beijing. This was the first time we had met either of them although we had conversed many times by telephone from England (usually in the middle of the night).

We had a long discussion, firstly about what they expected us to do for them whilst in China and then we moved on to more general matters about how Cadbury's was faring over here and how Jeff found life in China as a new resident. We had dinner together and then went back to our hotel for a round-up talk with another Jeff, the local Cadbury's representative.

We telephoned Children in Crisis and obtained their permission to publicly announce at the next day's press conference that we would be contributing a few thousand pounds to a Chinese charity (run by the Prime Minister's brother). This charity would be establishing an orphanage in the region. Fortunately Jeff also agreed that Cadbury's would pay for all our telephone calls back home!

The sunlight streamed through the window and woke me at 4 a.m. the next morning. I dozed for a while but still went down for an early breakfast. We cleaned the car and put it on display on the hotel forecourt. A press conference was held just inside the foyer, which was well attended and seemed to go down well. I certainly enjoyed myself. By this time Cadbury's had arranged for my videotapes to be relayed on to a master tape. This was then played back as a background at each press conference. I must admit that, at least in parts, the tape gave a very good indication of the atmosphere along the route and of the difficulties we faced in terms of poor road surfaces. It also showed well the challenging detours that we had to take through fields when the road was completely blocked with abandoned maintenance machinery or oversized boulders. The soundtrack also picked up nicely the noise of stones smashing against the skid shield.

Our next leg of the journey was to Changchun. We were assured that the roads from here on were all of good quality and the distance to Changchun was such that it should only take us about four hours. We had a leisurely lunch and left at 2 p.m.

En route a rather smart car overtook us, with a male driver and two attractive girls in the back. They were fascinated with the Healey and insisted on driving directly in front of us. The girls opened the sunroof and stood up, blowing kisses at us and generally being very friendly. Yet again this wasn't the sort of response I had anticipated from

160

the Chinese! After some miles they indicated that they were going to pull in for something to eat and drink. We followed them and the six of us had a snack together at a roadside café. We spent an hour or so talking with them. They were nurses at the local hospital and were full of fun. We said our goodbyes and continued onwards. They roared ahead of us but half an hour later we found them at the side of the road and they waved us down. They had bought us huge bags of fruit and other delicacies as a present. Again, this wasn't what I had expected from the Chinese.

The roads were now of excellent quality. This was the first time since we had left Germany all those weeks ago that we had seen anything like the conditions that one comes to expect as a matter of routine in England. However, just as the quality of the roads improved so too did the density of the traffic. It was surprising just how swiftly the terrain changed from being truly rural with little habitation except for within the villages and occasional large cities, to a scene which became one long urban sprawl. We arrived in Changchun at 8 p.m. Changchun is a large industrial city. Our hotel, inspiringly named the Chanchun Hotel, was superb. We were immediately introduced to the manager, who made all his staff line up to greet us. The Healey was given the pride of place on a pedestal just in front of the main doors. What a welcome!

Our stay in Changchun, however, was brief and we were off again early the next morning, heading for Shenyang. I had hardly heard of these cities before leaving England yet most had populations well into the millions. We were escorted by one of the hotel staff, who rode ahead of us as a motorbike outrider all the way from the city centre hotel to the motorway entrance. We were now travelling at around 50 m.p.h. – the fastest we had motored for many weeks. We lapped up the miles.

As we were travelling through the town of Gongzhuling we passed a schoolhouse where we saw that the annual school photograph was about to be taken. We discussed this as we drove past and decided to pull up and reverse for a closer look. As we neared the school gates the teachers waved for us to come in. We parked the car just inside the gates and were asked to sit in the front row for the school photograph! Our arrival created a great deal of excitement at this small village school. The headmistress asked if we would like to look round the school and we were taken to see the two main classrooms. The walls were quite bare and the desks were very basic but the enthusiasm of the children was evident for all to see. They were very polite. As soon as we entered the room this class of seven- to nine-year-olds stood up and waited in silence. JinBo gave a short speech in Chinese explaining who we were and there was a rowdy round of applause. The children then put on a little play-cum-song for us which lasted about ten minutes. We were then ushered into the senior class, where much the same happened but we also had a ten-minute discussion where the children asked about life in England. It was fascinating. In as much as one could glean anything in half an hour, I did find that the pupils were well educated on world current affairs. We were then taken into the headmistress's office and, accompanied by her three senior staff members, we had quite a lengthy talk about the comparison of life in general and teaching methods in particular between China and England. Fortunately my wife was a teacher so I had learnt a little bit about the English system from her and was able to converse with some authority on the subject (but, admittedly, not much!). Yet again I was surprised as I realised just how keen they were to know about England and how free they were to talk about the good points and what they perceived as the bad points in their own education system. We were given tea, coffee and, of all things, ice lollipops! We spent a good couple of hours on this impromptu stop and I found it a fascinating insight into the school life of the Chinese, at least in this region of the country. We never did get a copy of the school photograph though!

We stopped later for lunch and, as usual, when we came out of the restaurant there was a crowd of about 100 people surrounding the car. After many individual conversations, as they all were keen to try out their English, we set off again, with everyone in a good mood.

Since we had left Russia there had been less pressure. This earlier pressure had kept the adrenaline going and, probably, was therefore exactly what we needed to overcome the various hitches. However, the China leg of our trip was all in all more enjoyable. It was quite simply good fun. It was also fascinating to see a completely different culture at first hand. We were, of course, still travelling through areas where very few foreigners had ever been. The tourist trade, now an important earner of foreign exchange for China, just hadn't been developed this far north.

Nawal also seemed in better humour now that the pressure of Russia was behind us. I got to thinking that he probably was one of the few people that I would have partnered on a trip like this. I still thought of him as a very self-centred and determined character, but if that was my only complaint after six weeks then it was a minor problem. His tenacity and undoubted negotiating skills had been invaluable. In addition, he had been more positive than me in trying new ideas. One example occurred only that morning – the stop at the village school. It had been his idea, whereas I would probably have noted the scene but driven straight on. It had turned out to be a superb experience, one that I would be unlikely to repeat ever again. My conclusion remained that given our very different characters, it was surprising just how well we had got on and how few our actual arguments had been.

The remaining journey was uneventful and we reached Shenyang on schedule at 5 p.m. We were again greeted by the whole complement of hotel staff and, to the amusement of literally hundreds of passers-by, were the subject of another press photo call organised by the Cadbury team.

We were entertained to dinner by the very jovial crowd from the PR team. Plenty of *kanpai*s – the cry given when making a toast. They were all fond of a particular Chinese

163

wine-based liqueur, very sweet but very strong! We had quite a few of those before dinner was over and we fell into our beds again back at the hotel.

The next morning was 4 July – American Independence Day, but nobody recognised it as such. We had to call Radio 5 again later that day as well as Chris Capstick in Birmingham. We were hoping to move on as soon as possible to Tianjin – our last stop before Beijing. We knew that we had a press conference that morning and were hoping to do a little sightseeing that afternoon, but a mid-afternoon departure should still get us to Tianjin by evening. We were rather in the hands of the PR team, however, who quite rightly wanted to get as much out of our presence as possible for Cadbury's benefit. As they were now paying all the bills, who was I to object? Besides, I was really enjoying the experience of China.

The morning press conference went very well. The PR team had organised it as professionally as usual. A word on the general format of the press conferences might be of interest. We held a total of six when we were in China. Each was in an hotel room and anything from about a dozen to three dozen media people accepted the invitations to attend. It was therefore quite a large affair, considering that we were hardly world news. Nawal and I plus the key personnel in the PR team plus the senior people in the Cadbury team, i.e. a total of perhaps eight people, would be seated at the head of the room. Behind us would be a large and very smart-looking board which gave the details of the trip, including our names in Chinese and English. There would be the opportunity for slides to be screened to one side to illustrate a particular point raised and on a large TV screen on the other side my video typically would be played throughout the proceedings. The Chairman of Cadbury's would give an opening speech explaining why they supported ventures like ours and would take the opportunity to describe what they were doing in China. Then JinBo would stand up and give a commentary on the logistics of the trip so far and would recount a couple of anecdotes about particular incidents. Then there would be questions from the floor. These would go on for perhaps half an hour and would, typically, be split 50/50 between questions about the specific detail of the trip and our impression of China. One must remember the sheer scale of China's population. Most of the cities we travelled through had more than sufficient people to justify several local newspapers and, often, a local TV station. Frequently we saw ourselves in the next day's press and on the local TV news.

It surprised me at first just how much interest was being shown in our trip. I suppose that it was because it was a little different and, as we now know, it was in fact unique. I think the Chinese are particularly interested in the activities of the few non-tourist foreigners in their midst as they are, of course, very sensitive to the image that is portrayed of them in the international media. They were only too well aware that they had often been heavily criticised for abuse of human rights.

I remember that one of the functions we attended before we left England was a civic dinner held in St Albans – Nawal's home town. Several hundred people attended. The guest speaker was the former Archbishop of Canterbury – Robert Runcie. Part of the purpose of our attendance was to raise the profile of our trip and the mayor was kind enough to give us quite a lengthy mention in his speech. As a result of that the Archbishop made a point of coming over to see us after the official speeches and expressed a great interest in our imminent journey. He himself had visited China fairly recently. I remember him saying words to the effect that: 'People in the West have no idea of the scale of the problems in China. Here is the world's largest country with, perhaps, one and a half billion people. They have huge social problems and also the most basic problem of all – the difficulty of becoming self-sufficient in food in order to feed their people. They have to take drastic steps in fairness to all. That is why they have, quite understandably, introduced the "one child per family" policy. It really is the right thing to do in the extreme circumstances in which they

165

find themselves and yet they are pilloried by the West for undemocratic compulsion.'

We didn't travel further that day after all but instead were taken on a fascinating conducted tour of Shenyang's Forbidden City.

We set off very early the following morning and took a packed breakfast with us. Tianjin was 450 miles away but we hoped to make it by the early evening. The roads were generally very good but there remained several stretches 'under repair'. We passed the city of Jinzhou around mid-day, and as this had originally been considered as our next overnight stop, we felt we were making very good progress and should still be in Tianjin by evening.

It was beginning to get very hot. We had been travelling virtually due south consistently throughout the last few days. We had been told that the temperature in Beijing had reached 100 degrees Fahrenheit on the previous day.

We stopped for a late lunch in the town of Xiangchang and ordered five dishes from a local restaurant but still ended up with several more, for some reason. Fortunately it started to rain in the afternoon and this significantly helped to make us feel a little better. The outside temperature had been over 90 degrees so I dread to think what the interior temperature had been. We had all been feeling dehydrated despite many liquid intake stops.

The day wore on and the last 100 miles was slow going, partly because of heavy traffic. We were still far enough away from Beijing for the normal traffic to include donkeys, shepherds with flocks of geese, bicycles, of course, and slow-moving heavy lorries. We eventually arrived at the four-star Geneva Hotel in Tianjin at midnight. We all felt really drained but were sustained with the thought that that was the last long run of the whole trip. In fact the final leg to Beijing was only 125 miles.

On Saturday we spent a very interesting day in Tianjin. In the morning we were taken to an orphanage in the centre of the city which had been established ten years ago. It was part of the SOS International organisation formed in Austria in 1949. A team from Switzerland regularly inspected the orphanage. I was very impressed with the quality of the staff and the system whereby the complex was designed as a group of large houses on a campus. Each house is seen as a family unit. Children are taken in from the age of zero up to about ten years old and usually stay until their late teens. They are assigned to a house which holds a maximum of eight children. Each house is run by a 'mother' and about the only criterion that was common to all the mothers that we met was that they must not be 'real' mothers. In other words, they were expected to dedicate themselves on a permanent basis to act as a parent to the children in their particular house. I was still a little wary that the Chinese, with an eye on their international image, would show us only what they wanted us to see. That remark does nothing to detract from my earlier good impressions because most of the people we had met and the things we had done so far were impromptu. The children we saw at the orphanage were all quite amazing. They were extremely polite, but that is a trait we found everywhere with Chinese children. They were all talented in different ways. We were introduced to a very confident six-year-old boy who played a xylophone for us as though he were truly in a professional orchestra. He was as fast as lightning. I was later told that when he was only five he had represented China at some Far Eastern music festival in Korea. We saw others, including a seven-year-old girl who was a most talented dancer. We were then escorted to the principal's room, where he welcomed us most profusely and spent an hour or so explaining how the orphanage was run. It was a fascinating experience.

In the afternoon we held another press conference back at the hotel, which followed the same format as before. I was again surprised by just how well these meetings were attended. There was a full hour of questioning after the presentation so we didn't finish until after 6 p.m. I then had a rare couple of hours entirely to myself. This was a luxury. I telephoned home to find that all was well and then,

167

prompted by the heat, went out to get my hair cut. At about 8 p.m. the local Cadbury manager took us out to see the local 'food street'. It covered several streets, in fact, and every conceivable type of food was on sale. This included many live animals as well as exotic fruits, sweets and cakes, fish and a huge range of herbs and spices. We had dinner in a small and lively restaurant which gave us the authentic feel of the city.

I woke up on the Sunday excited that we were about to make our final run. I also thought a lot about the support I was getting from back home. Every time I telephoned, Jenny told me that things were fine and that I should make the most of this trip. I am sure that all sorts of things had gone wrong, as they always do in a busy household, but not once had Jenny burdened me with any domestic problems. I was very mindful of that and thought she really was good to have encouraged me throughout.

The only bad news that morning was that my blue Rohan trousers seemed to have been lost by the hotel laundry service. Although I had a spare pair, I had to admit that I had worn this pair on every single travelling day. I had occasionally rinsed them out at night but, given their light-weight material, they were always dry in readiness for wear the next day. They had become real friends. I was very sad to see the last of them. (Given these remarks about a pair of trousers – you can just tell how one's mind begins to go after several weeks with few possessions!)

Jerry Zhou was regularly concerned with the amount of expenses that we were running up. I guess a phone call home would be costly and we were staying at first-class hotels (albeit at Cadbury's insistence). As a regional Cadbury's manager, we later learnt that he earned only about $100 to $150 per month, so it was understandable that he might query the fact that we seemed to manage to spend this amount in just one day. But I don't think we were prolific. After all, it was difficult to spend less, given that Cadbury's chose the hotels and restaurants for us. I suppose that's why we didn't give him much sympathy and simply said that that was his problem. Poor Jerry – I guess he would just have to sell a few hundred more chocolate bars in order to make up his budget!

I was concerned that the whole trip was likely to cost me several thousand pounds, whereas I had hoped to find that sponsorship had covered all my expenses. But I soon realised the meanness and folly of that thought. We had been away for seven weeks enjoying sights that most people could only dream about. I would have paid that price many times over if I had to, just to be able to have experienced all the fabulous moments of the last few weeks. I felt that our journey really had lived up to its billing as a unique trip of a lifetime.

We completed a number of tasks as requested by Cadbury's such as a mini photo session with a photographer who had been unable to make it to the previous day's press conference.

I suffered a minor eye infection and that made me think just how lucky we had both been. Apart from my scalded arm, neither of us had suffered any accident or illness of note. Not bad, considering the weeks we had been battling it out together. In fact, I think I felt healthier throughout the trip than I had done for a long time. My diet had been good and was probably a key factor. In China there were few sweet foodstuffs available, nor much in the way of milk, butter or dairy produce in general. We typically ate vegetables, which were usually pickled, even for breakfast. Meat, fish dishes and rice were predominant. No puddings, sweets, chocolate, cheese, crisps or gin and tonics – the sort of things that I loved and were my downfall in England.

The last lap to Beijing was even shorter than expected, being expressway all the way. When we recognised the Chinese symbols that denoted the city limit of Beijing, we got out of the car to have our photograph taken. The literal translation of these two symbols is 'North' and 'Capital', which reminded us just how big the country was. We had been driving due south for several days and we were still very much in the north of the country.

By this time we were regularly travelling with at least one other vehicle – usually the PR team's van – so that when it came to taking photographs there was always somebody on hand to be able to take Nawal, JinBo and me together – this time under the Beijing City sign. This was our official finishing line, I suppose, as our trip had been billed as London to Beijing. We were, nevertheless, looking forward to a drive around Tiananmen Square right in the centre of the capital in a couple of days' time.

We took a long time to drive through the suburbs to our hotel. When we got there the management team would not allow us to park near the hotel entrance. Nawal and I stood to one side as a great deal of negotiation went on. Eventually, though, as no compromise was reached, we were advised that we were going to find another hotel. This we did. We moved to the superb Continental Hotel which was located adjacent to the site of the recent Asian Games. Apparently this had been JinBo's first choice so he was pleased. JinBo's boss, the gregarious Mr Lee, had joined the party by now. He seemed to be a man with some authority. He arranged for the car to be parked in pride of place, right in front of the main hotel doors. We were allocated a room on the sixteenth floor which had a wonderful view of the city.

We spent the next four days in Beijing. It was a hectic period. We had a visit from Will Burgess, Mark O'Neil and Tom Kirkland who represented the local office of Reuters. They were going to do a bit of a story on us and wanted to film us driving round Tiananmen Square. We discussed the details of this event, which was scheduled for the following day.

JinBo took us to see the Great Wall and it was fun driving the Healey through the bridge underneath the wall. Like most people, I had heard a lot about it and it is certainly an impressive sight. The statistic I remember from my schooldays is that it is the last manmade object you would see on earth if you were departing in a space rocket, such is its overall size. However, my abiding memory is one of disappointment. Having seen few tourists throughout the last couple of months, we suddenly came across the Great Wall car park, which must have contained a hundred tourist coaches. The wall itself was difficult to see because of the massive number of foreign visitors. Literally hundreds of Japanese, Americans, Germans, English and, no doubt, just about every other nationality were swarming all over it. There is, of course, no reason why anyone shouldn't be allowed to visit the wall, but to see this historic sight so crowded and to see the inevitable tourist support facilities such as hamburger bars, souvenir stalls, buskers and touts of every description, just took the edge off it for me. I guess that I felt like this because I had been so spoilt having just seen many of the world's beauty spots without another soul to be seen.

Further press conferences ensued. We also did quite a bit of promotional work for Cadbury's. At one point the front doors of a huge showpiece supermarket were unhinged in order to let us take the car inside. We parked in the central atrium and displayed posters describing our trip, with my inevitable video playing alongside. Cadbury's distributed their chocolates. It was staggering just to see the sheer number of people who were interested. We had a queue all day long who were prepared to pay $5 (not an inconsiderable sum for many Chinese) just to have their photographs taken with either Nawal or me sitting alongside them in the car. (The money was given to a local charity.)

Our Tiananmen Square drive fully lived up to expectations. I had been in Red Square in Moscow which is the nearest comparison I could make. But Tiananmen is just so much bigger. I could well imagine the famous scene just five years before when the students physically stood in the way of the People's Liberation Army tanks as they held their peaceful protest against the then regime. It had been a very brave thing to do. I could sense the awe-inspiring atmosphere of the square. A huge poster of Chairman Mao Tse-tung stared down at us from the northern end. We drove round the square about six times until Reuters were satisfied with the shoot.

We did plenty of sightseeing and enjoyed many delicious meals out. There are, of course, several different and distinct regions in China, each with their own style of food. We were introduced to a number of restaurants that specialised in one or other of these regional delicacies. We even went to a snake restaurant but I wouldn't recommend it to the squeamish, unless keen to eat a snake immediately after seeing it being skinned alive! Even I lost my appetite on that evening.

On the Wednesday night we were entertained at a very rowdy and highly successful dinner by the whole of the Beijing team. This comprised Jeff Briggs, Ma Dan and about a dozen of the Cadbury people, plus half a dozen from the PR company. There seemed to be a goodly number of sundry hangers-on as well. All in all we must have numbered three dozen. It was a great evening with plenty of speeches and plenty of jokes.

We were also taken to see the Cadbury factory. This was a great deal more interesting than it sounds. It had only recently been constructed and was as clean as a whistle as well as being state-of-the-art. I felt that it provided a very attractive working environment for the Chinese who were employed there.

We visited a traditional Chinese acrobatic theatre, which proved to be an excellent form of entertainment. We went to see the Forbidden City – it really was marvellous to have JinBo with us most of the time. Not only had he proved to be a good friend and a great guy to be with, but as his main business was tourism in some form or other, he knew all the places to go. The fact that he could speak the language was a huge bonus. I bought a number of small souvenirs but had one eye on the very tight weight limit for luggage that I would be allowed to bring home on the aeroplane.

I finally left Beijing on Thursday, 11 July. I said goodbye to Nawal, who was going to stay on for an extra couple of days and get a visa to visit his home country of India for a short spell before flying to England. He also had to complete arrangements for the car to be shipped home to Harwich.

JinBo and two PR men took me to the airport. We crawled through the early morning commuter traffic and when we got there it was a lengthy process just to check in. On top of that, the flight was delayed a couple of hours 'for technical reasons'. However, at least I was well used to delays for technical reasons by now. The flight was uneventful and took just 11 hours to London's Heathrow airport. When the captain announced the route we would be taking I found that all the names were familiar to me. We were going to fly over the exact same route for the next 11 hours that we had taken seven weeks to cross overland in the other direction. I confess to feeling somewhat nostalgic as he gave us the names of the cities that we would be flying over: Shenyang, Harbin, Irkutsk, Novosibirsk, Omsk, Moscow, Minsk – I knew every one!

Given the time difference, I arrived in England in late afternoon that same day. Everywhere looked lush and rich and neat. I kept thinking of the charity team working against the odds in Belarus, of Alexei and family who had 'saved our lives' and been our hosts in their tiny Siberian village, and of the very many people whom we had come across during the previous couple of months. At home I was given a marvellous reception and found that Jenny had organised a surprise welcome party with all the people that had waved us off a few weeks earlier. It had been a fabulous trip but it was really great to be back home!

Since completing this trip I do find that it has changed me, as all life's experiences tend to do. Of course this particular 'experience' or 'odyssey', to give it a more accurate description, had been particularly fascinating. The main reason for putting my experiences of the trip down on paper is to encourage anyone – regardless of age or experience – who has half a mind to do something similar. You would be amazed just how much you would benefit from taking up a challenge similar to this. It was so much more rewarding and, ultimately, self-satisfying than anything I had ever experienced before.

Many of the moments that we enjoyed (or suffered!) will remain in my memory forever. Despite all my initial apprehensions and my recognition of the fact that I had no special skills that equipped me for a trip like this, I had had the time of my life. I truly wouldn't have missed it for the world. It was fabulous.

I have subsequently given a number of talks to various local groups, and people there often ask me whether I have learnt anything in particular from my experiences. The answer is most certainly yes. Of the many thoughts that cross my mind I think that there are two things that stand out.

The first and foremost is that despite differences of history, religion, language, lifestyles and political systems, I found that most ordinary people have far more in common with each other than some of our world leaders would have us believe: a common sense of decency, a love and responsibility for family and friends and even a similar sense of humour. The media, through the reporting of world news, seem to feed us an unending diet of gloom. Throughout our journey we met very many different characters and everyone was unfailingly friendly and unstintingly helpful. As a result, this trip restored my faith in humanity.

The second thing I have learnt is that I can now truly claim to be the world's leading expert on Austin Healey exhaust systems!

ROUTING DETAILS

26 May 1996   Bishop's Stortford, Herts, to Harwich
Overnight Stena Line Ferry (*Konnigen Beatrix*) to Hook of Holland

27 May   Motorway E25 Rotterdam, E30 Utrecht, Amersfoort, Apeldoorn, Enschede, Osnabrück, Hannover, Magdeburg, Berlin, POLAND, Swiebodzin (Hotel Lubuski)

28 May   Pniewy, Poznan, Konin, Lowicz, Warsaw (Hotel Europejski)

29 May   stay Warsaw

30 May   stay Warsaw

31 May   BELARUS, Brest, Minsk (Hotel Planeta)

1 June   stay Minsk

2 June   stay Minsk

3 June   Borisov, Orsha, RUSSIA, Smolensk (Motel Phoenix)

4 June   Safonovo, Vyazma, Gagarin, Moscow (Hotel Gorbachov)

5 June   stay Moscow

6 June   Noginsk, Vladimir, Kovrov, Nizhniy Novgorod (Hotel Rusia)

7 June   Cheboksary, Kazan, Brezhnev, Ufa

8 June   Zlatoust, Miaz, Chelyabinsk

9 June   Shadrinsk, Tyumen

10 June   Ishin, Omsk

11 June   KAZAKSTAN, RUSSIA, Karasuk, Kamen, Novosibirsk (Hotel Sibir then flat of Maria's parents)

12 June   stay Novosibirsk

175

13 June	stay Novosibirsk
14 June	stay Novosibirsk
15 June	Yurga, Kemerovo (Andreev's flat)
16 June	Krasnoyarsk
17 June	stay Krasnoyarsk
18 June	stay Krasnoyarsk
19 June	Kansk, Tulun (guest house)
20 June	Zima, Cheremkhovo, Angarsk, Irkutsk (Hotel Intourist)
21 June	stay Irkutsk
22 June	Ulan-Ude (Hotel Buraije)
23 June	Chita (Hotel Dauria)
24 June	Olovyannaya (Home of Alexei)
25 June	Zabaykalsk (Flat of Valery)
26 June	CHINA, Manzhouli (Sinotrans Hotel)
27 June	stay Manzhouli
28 June	Hailar, Yakeshi (Hotel Yakeshi Lunchang)
29 June	Qiqihar (Hubin Hotel)
30 June	Daqing, Zandong, Harbin (Modern Hotel)
1 July	stay Harbin
2 July	Dehui, Changchun (Changchun Hotel)
3 July	Siping, Tieling, Shenyang (Hotel Rose)
4 July	stay Shenyang
5 July	Fuxin, Jinzhou, Tianjin (Geneva Hotel)
6 July	stay Tianjin
7 July	Beijing (Continental Hotel)
8 July	stay Beijing
9 July	stay Beijing
10 July	stay Beijing
11 July	Beijing (Air China flight CA937) London Heathrow

Total mileage:	8,003 (12,805 kilometres)
Fuel consumption:	1,509 litres (5.3 miles or 8.4 kilometres per litre)
Stopovers:	1 ferry, 4 Poland, 3 Belarus, 23 Russia, 12 China

ACKNOWLEDGEMENTS

It is important to thank all those people without whose help and assistance this trip would have been totally impossible.

On a personal note I would like to thank Nawal, not least for putting up with me and my many failings for seven weeks. It couldn't have been easy for him! I have tried to be honest – portraying him, his weaknesses as well as his strengths, as I saw them at the time. In the end I remain of the view that this trip was a most fabulous experience and without Nawal's tenacity, diplomacy and cool-headedness it would never have been completed.

I would like to thank all our many sponsors who contributed cash, equipment or time in the preparatory period before we set off. I would single out our lead sponsor Cadbury's; especially Chris Capstick based in Birmingham (who had responsibilities for the old Soviet bloc) for his enthusiasm throughout.

My thanks to Robert Narojek and his team in Poland and for the professionalism of their PR support team Euro-RSCG, who looked after us so well.

Also to Peter Kirby and his team in Moscow and their PR support team United Campaigns, particularly Victoria Ushakova for her efforts in arranging a string of contacts for us in Siberia.

Thanks too to Jeff Briggs and Ma Dan and the rest of the Cadbury's China team, including Jerry Zhou. To Mr Chung of the PR team for his support and jovial presence. To Mr Li at the Golden Friendship Travel team, without whose efforts to secure the 23 governmental permissions our entry into China would have been impossible.

My especial thanks to JinBo, our interpreter and 'Red Army spy' and now my very good friend. JinBo managed his own world first by being the only person to travel 2,500 miles in the cramped conditions of the rear seat of an Austin Healey!

Thanks also to the various Cadbury distribution agencies throughout, including Nino and Vadym in Minsk.

Thanks too to the Children of Crisis team in London, who were very enthusiastic and gave us a lot of help: Deborah Oxley, Juliet Smith and Claire Lewis.

Thanks too to the many charity workers whom we met en route and whose dedication to their causes made us feel very humble. In particular to Valentina of the Children of Chernobyl charity in Belarus.

Thanks also to all those many individuals and companies who donated money through us in order to improve the lives of many disadvantaged and underprivileged children.

Thanks also to all those people who have given us moral support and encouragement along the way.

My very special thanks and love to my other half, Jenny. She was a huge supporter of the idea throughout and she was absolutely correct with her original view that it was just what I needed to do at that stage in my life. Very perceptive!

Finally a huge thank you to those who will never hear the conclusion of our trip and the good it has done. Nor will I ever see them again. This is to the many ordinary citizens of Poland, Belarus, Russia and China who unfailingly gave us help whenever we required it and as a result restored my faith in humanity.